The COMPLETE FILMS of CHARLIE CHAPLIN

The COMPLETE FILMS of CHARLIE CHAPLIN

by
GERALD D. McDONALD,
MICHAEL CONWAY,
and MARK RICCI

THE CITADEL PRESS
Secaucus, New Jersey

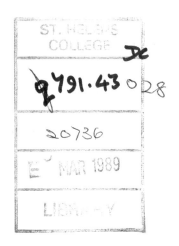
ACKNOWLEDGMENTS

The authors are grateful for all those who helped them obtain the photographs reproduced in this book: The Museum of Modern Art, New York; the Theatre Collection of The New York Public Library; the British Film Institute; Davide Turconi of Cinematigrafico, Pavia, Italy; John Kobal, the late Carlos Clarens, Dion McGregor, William K. Everson and Kevin Brownlow. We also wish to thank Harcourt, Brace & World, Inc., for permission to quote the lines of E. E. Cummings from *Poems 1923-1954*.

Contents

CHARLIE:
One of Nature's Own Naturals

GERALD D. McDONALD

i will cultivate within
me scrupulously the Inimitable which
is loneliness . . .

E. E. CUMMINGS

Upon the completion of Charlie Chaplin's first film, the officers of the Keystone Company were pessimistic, Mack Sennett was bewildered, and Henry Lehrman, the director of the film, was furious with the new actor. Chaplin himself was wondering if it would not be wiser to return to the stage.

Some months before this, Mack Sennett and Mabel Normand had seen Fred Karno's London Comedians in "A Night in an English Music Hall." When Ford Sterling later gave notice that he was leaving the Keystone Company, they both thought of the funny man who had played the "Inebriated Swell" in this skit. He seemed a likely replacement for Sterling, but they did not remember his name or know where he was then playing. Eventually, Charles Spencer Chaplin was located and signed at $150 a week. Through the gates of the Keystone Studio the twenty-five-year-old comedian entered the movies.

This event, which has turned out to be so important to motion pictures and to our culture, occurred more than a half-century ago. Chaplin, who was to become "the greatest theatrical artist of our time," the "most familiar human figure in the world," first appeared in films early in the year 1914. As the villain of a one-reel comedy, his costume was distinguished by a frock coat, a top hat, a drooping mustache, and a monocle. The film, called *Making a Living*, was a typical Keystone comedy of frenzied disorder, an exercise in skulduggery which inevitably led to a chase. It was made with a minor cast, except for Chester Conklin in a small role, and with a director who already considered the film to be a flop.

A New York writer for the *Moving Picture World* was assigned to review *Making a Living*. Chaplin's name was unknown to him; his name, unfortunately, is unknown to us. But he should be honored as the author of the first published appraisal of Chaplin as a film actor. The anonymous writer spotted a new performer on the screen, an agile rogue who kept up a running fire of comic business aided by his monocle, cane, and detachable cuffs. It was all "fresh and unexpected fun" to him. "The clever actor who takes the role of the nervy and very nifty sharper in this picture," he wrote, "is a comedian of the first water, who acts like one of Nature's own naturals."

Before this extraordinary review could bring comfort to the studio or exert any influence to have the characterization repeated in further films, the Little Tramp had come upon the scene. From his memories of men seen on London streets and on the stages of its music halls, Chaplin had a moment of inspiration which we can accept but cannot explain. From it came the invention of his screen character: what he was to wear; how he was to walk; what were to be his reactions to the outrageous fortunes of the comic world. Somehow he was able to settle this by the time he made his second film, *Kid Auto Races at Venice*.

In this first glimpse of the Little Tramp, Charlie was not yet wistful—but he was quite wonderful. The vagrant with the baggy trousers, derby, big shoes, and cane was a buffoon, notable at first for his acrobatic skill in falling, skidding, and delivering, in infinite variety, a swift and well-aimed kick. There was precision in his tricks and postures, a great store of invention in the fun he brought to comic villainy. In good time he would become the medium of expression for his creator's ideas and feelings. He would remain a creature of comedy, but in the deepening sadness of life he would eventually express its tragedy. He would become the lonely outcast in whom we found the predicaments of modern man.

But those first months in 1914 were full of uncertainty both for Chaplin and for Keystone. If Chaplin had to find his own way to express himself on film, Mack Sennett and his associates had to come to terms with the fact that they had a star who could not take direction. Chaplin needed freedom if he was to be at his best. While he worked and chafed under other directors, he knew, and it was soon realized at Keystone, that he must become his own director and prepare the stories he was to use. Sennett said Chaplin once asked him, "If you want somebody to pull all of the old gags, why did you hire me?"

Left to his own devices, Charlie was as full of dough and dynamite as the other Keystone comics, and his little films were full of fun. But Chaplin tried to make everything he did "a burlesque on something in real life." "Comedy must be real and true to life," he said.

It was his audience, rather than studio publicity, that was responsible for Chaplin's unprecedented rise to fame. Filmgoers found him overwhelmingly funny and were delighted with what they saw long before the Little Tramp, as we think of him now, was completely revealed. They were usually quite untroubled by his rascality. Wasn't it Gilbert Seldes who said that people accepted it as they might accept an insulting phrase in a will which was to bring them a fortune?

Chaplin spent a year at the Keystone Studio, where he made thirty-five comedies, including that famous six-reel laugh fest, *Tillie's Punctured Romance*. Then came the year at Essanay, and the ever-increasing fame. He was aware that his worldwide audiences were making him their idol, but this may only have deepened his own sense of loneliness.

His earlier films came to a world filled with anxieties and wartime tensions. In the search for moments of diversion, for something to take their minds off the war, people found Charlie. With his magic cane he made the sad old world, for a moment, a very funny place. He did almost as much to internationalize the American film as did the war. If World War I slowed down European production to a point where American films were needed, the Chaplin comedies raised their popularity to the point where they were *wanted*. Charlie—Charlot, Carlos, Carlito—was welcomed by children and by the young in heart. Intellectuals discovered him and rediscovered him, as if Charlie were suffering from neglect and they must tell people about this wonderful comedian. Burton Rascoe once reminded these writers that "the appreciative public" had been roundly applauding his work for a long time and had paid enough money for the privilege to make Chaplin a millionaire.

The delight Charlie gave and the affection he inspired may have had their roots in folk memory. Europe has always had a high appreciation of the clown and recognized that here was a clown in the great tradition. But there was also a sense of recognition, perhaps, which reached further into the twilight of the past. Before Chaplin became the universal "little man," he was the Trickster. In the Keystone comedies, and at certain times in all of his later pictures, he was the simpleton who was also a clever rogue, with talents near to genius in useless endeavors but inept and bungling in what he was supposed to do. Charlie was the mischief-maker, Till Eulenspiegel of the merry pranks. He was the fool, sometimes gullible and stupid, sometimes impudent and cunning, displaying a high degree of effrontery and chicanery. His misadventures echoed stories known all over the world: the trickster tales, which have been among the ones best liked.

Charlie himself entered folklore during the World War I years. Marching soldiers sang to the tune of "Red Wing," "Oh, the moon shines bright on Charlie Chaplin." Children soon made the song their own, then set about creating others—"Charlie Chaplin went to France, To teach the ladies how to dance." In their counting games they chanted, "Charlie Chaplin sat on a pin, How many inches did it go in?" In Puerto Rico children sang a little song warning anyone who had a kitten to keep it indoors, for "Chali Chaplin" would come along and hit it with his cane. In England, too, children recognized his roguery when they sang, to the strains of "Gentle Jesus,"

Charlie Chaplin meek and mild
Took a sausage from a child.
When the child began to cry
Charlie slapped him in the eye.

By the time he joined the Essanay Company in 1915, Chaplin was already feeling the burden of fame. "What difference does it make," he asked an interviewer, "whether I eat mustard with ice cream or put sugar in beer, except on the screen?" But he could not escape the spotlight. As one looks back on Chaplin's career the spectre of Public Attention, so gratifying in many of its manifestations, becomes something disturbing and abusive. The attacks on Chaplin were first directed to what many considered the vulgarities of his early films. "Accompanying the funny things that Mr. Chaplin does are some incredible infractions of the proprieties," wrote Percy Hammond in 1915. "I have seen Mr. Chaplin blithely performing functions in the moving pictures that even I would decline to report."

Next came the complaints of exhibitors, who felt they had to pay too much for Chaplin's films, and were obliged to take pictures they did not want in order to get the Chaplins. In the war years he was criticized by those who felt he was not "doing his bit" in the common cause. As his salary soared to tremendous heights, grumblings were heard from people who were offended when they compared his earnings with those of the President of the United States. Then came the legal battles of his divorces from Mildred Harris and Lita Grey. Later there were attacks on his alleged Shakespearean freedom in the use of material claimed by others, further publicity on his relations with women, and the most severe censure of his ideological enthusiasms. Chaplin has had a great career, perhaps the greatest in films, but it has been a troubled one.

In writing about Charlie Chaplin, two personalities are involved, the man, Chaplin, and the created character, Charlie. We must follow *Charlie* through all of his films to discover *his* personality and to find how wide it was in range. The complete image was not fully expressed in any one film, not even in *The Gold Rush*. In that superb film, which almost shows Charlie complete, the important note of rebellion and nonconformity was not struck. That aspect was shown best, perhaps, in the wonderful opening to *City Lights,* when the formal unveiling of the civic monument discloses the Little Tramp asleep on the lap of one of the great stone figures.

We most often think of Charlie as the one who loses, as the one whose hopes must go down in defeat. Charlie first showed us this side of his nature, and of his destiny, in *The Tramp*. The beautiful, ambiguous ending of *City Lights* must be interpreted in this way, as a moment of tragic loss when Charlie stands before the girl who has gained her sight through his efforts. He is giving her the full measure of his devotion, whereas the girl, seeing him as he really is for the first time, offers him that most insufficient gift, her gratitude.

If Charlie was to be the winner, it was often only in a dream, as in *The Bank, Shoulder Arms* or *The Idle Class*. Sometimes the mere ability to make an escape was victory enough. There were films, however, in which he knew what he wanted and got it through trickery, following the pattern set by *Making a Living*. When a genuinely happy ending occurred, as it did in *The Gold Rush, The Vagabond,* and *Sunnyside,* it came as the reward of innocence. We dubiously accepted it as a fantasy we wanted very much to believe.

Charlie Chaplin was a part of the early youth of the movies and he grew as they grew. The art of the film lives only as long as it grows; so does the art of a great comedian. When the Little Tramp was left behind and Chaplin turned to *The Great Dictator, Monsieur Verdoux,* and *Limelight,* it was a change that was necessary to Chaplin and to the times in which the films were made. He recognized the sad fact that films could no longer accommodate pure pantomime, that the wilder shores of slapstick had somehow become submerged. The old subjects of public laughter had become narrowed, but new subjects were possible. He was a pioneer in the present trend to find fun in the unfunny: the Depression, the Nazi menace, and murder as a means of "making a living."

In his first departure from his familiar comedy, *A Woman of Paris,* Chaplin undoubtedly felt an inner need to create a film which had no relation to his Tramp, but one to which he could give expression of all he had learned as a film-maker. The scene of that film may not have been particularly Parisian, but it was certainly not the world we had come to know through Charlie. That world is recalled in the illustrations to this book. A park bench in summertime, with shenanigans in the nearby bushes; a lake to fall in, to sink, but never quite to drown; a sea beach, a boardwalk, and always a hot-dog stand; pretty girls chaperoned by vigilant duennas or jealous husbands, and nearby, the omnipresent cop; a city of flophouses, saloons, and dance halls, with a street somewhere which always looks like old London; the ballrooms soon to be wrecked, the hotels already invaded; the lonesome roads for a lonely figure who has found he was not wanted. That was Charlie's land, and there he lived in comic desperation.

Never underestimate the wonder of Charlie's eyes as he looked upon these scenes. It was the eyes that helped make Charlie unique. No one has so successfully broken the rule of looking straight into the camera, and thus straight at us, the audience—especially when he was up to some mischief which he did not want his fellow actors to see. It was just a trick, perhaps, but it gave an added dimension to his films.

Chaplin captured on film the spirit of comedy. He has always known, or so it now seems, that comic art is profoundly serious. The Little Tramp did not know that he was funny, although he made the whole world laugh. There was no hint, unless it was in the last of the Little Tramp films, *Modern Times,* that an actor was calculating his effects or making a conscious effort to entertain. The artist's comment, of course, was always present, but it was made in the very essence of the Little Tramp's character and seemed never to be superimposed.

Chaplin's films, filled with the scenes we love to recall, contributed a dominant chapter to the history of the motion picture. They were important to the artistic development of American films and quite as important to their economic growth. If there should ever be a Motion Picture Hall of Fame, serious in its intent, it is impossible to believe that he would not be among the first to be chosen for it. The only thing worth noticing in the display of names now set into the sidewalks of Hollywood is the absence of the name of Charles Chaplin.

Chaplin's films are crowded with wonderful incidents, but their plots are no measure of their total effect. It is not what happens in the story that interests us, but what happens in Charlie. The synopses which we have attempted to give in these pages are merely an aid to recollection, a means of identifying a particular film. To see a Chaplin comedy, then to try to tell what you have seen, is a difficult thing to do.

The quoted criticisms of the films, written at the time of their release, are often rather curious. Film criticism had hardly begun when Chaplin's first films appeared. If a short comedy was mentioned at all, to say that it was funny seemed to suffice. The reviews often fail to say what we so much want them to say, and the writers sometimes seem oblivious to innovation, change, and growth. Some of the films which we would place among his weaker efforts were as well received as his best ones. The most remarkable of the early reviews is the one for his first film, when the writer immediately recognized a major talent, and a British review of the first of his Essanay films, in which the writer successfully analyzed what made Chaplin funny. It was the pioneer consideration of a subject which has never yet been exhausted.

The writers of the reviews were often obsessed by the vulgarities they found, and complained, not always grammatically, about the need for better stories. Yet these comments from scattered sources, British and American, sometimes display remarkable insights. And quite as important, we can sometimes come very close to the responses of the first audiences who beheld these films. Even the quotations from what we consider excellent reviews, made when film criticism had come of age, are not definitive. We are reminded of what Garcia Lorca once wrote about criticism. Works of art, he said (and there are sequences in Chaplin's films, sometimes complete films, that *are* works of art), stand so alone that they cannot be approached by criticism. They can only be approached by love.

A Bit About Chaplin and His Films

MICHAEL CONWAY

Charles Spencer Chaplin was born on April 16, 1889, in Walworth, a section of London, England. As an only child, he was named after his father, who died when Chaplin was a youngster. Both his parents were music hall entertainers. Sydney, his mother's son by a previous marriage, came to live with the Chaplins and took the Chaplin name. Sydney had a career of his own in films, but he did appear in Chaplin's First National comedies. Wheeler Dryden, one of his mother's two sons by another marriage, became associated with Chaplin in his later United Artists films.

Chaplin learned some vaudeville routines while still a toddler, but his first major professional work was as one of the "Eight Lancashire Lads," a group of preteenage boys who toured the music halls doing a dance act. He left the group when he was nine years old. He obtained jobs in stage plays, off and on, but his most important work came when he was seventeen years old. Through Sydney, who was working for Fred Karno, Chaplin obtained an interview with Karno and a job with his stage company. The Karno Company was actually a group of companies which were sent out to various areas to give comedy performances. Chaplin remained with the Karno Company for several years and built up a good name for himself as a performer.

In 1913, Chaplin was on tour with one of the Karno groups in the United States. Mack Sennett, head of the Keystone Studio in Los Angeles, saw Chaplin performing and had one of the officials of the studio invite him to talk about a film contract. Chaplin signed with Sennett for one year. By the end of 1914, Chaplin had appeared in thirty-five films.

The Keystone comedy shorts were made in a strange manner. Scripts were unnecessary in many of Sennett's films. If someone had an idea for a funny situation, and it was possible to film it, the camera rolled. Slapstick was comedy and comedy was slapstick. Sennett held to the theory that rough-and-tumble comedy had the most appeal. He kept to this idea right into the sound era, when the taste in comedy changed. Audiences ignored slapstick; Sennett did not. In 1938, Republic Pictures purchased the Sennett Studio.

The secret of Chaplin's success was his originality, and so he endured. At Keystone, however, he was at first in no position to work in his own way. He was just one of the Sennett Company. When he first worked with Mabel Normand, artistic temperaments clashed. Both had a fine sense of comedy and ideas on how a scene should be played. Although they had arguments at the beginning of their work together, they grew to respect one another's ability and even became friends. Chaplin, it soon became clear, was the stronger of the two so far as audience appeal was concerned. In the one year that Chaplin was at Keystone, he had established himself as one of the most popular comedians in films. He was no longer Charles Spencer Chaplin. He was Charlie—the little man with a mustache, carrying a cane and wearing a derby, who walked in such a way that you would think he was going straight ahead in two directions. He had a magic formula: he could identify himself with the common man.

Chaplin left Keystone to work at Essanay in 1915. He was no longer burdened by supervision and could develop his own treatment of comedy. He experimented with different types of humorous situations, sometimes incurring the anger of the critics of the day. Some of Chaplin's experiments were described as uncouth or just plain dirty.

These criticisms, however, did not affect his popularity.

Chaplin's Little Tramp character came into full bloom in his Essanay films, but he left this company when the Mutual Company offered him more money and better working conditions. Although he never worked for Essanay again after he departed its fold, that company released a comedy in 1918 called *Triple Trouble* as if it were a brand-new Chaplin comedy. In reality, however, it consisted of scenes from several of Chaplin's Essanays, although it did contain unused Chaplin Essanay footage as well. (This film is discussed in detail in this book.) The title could have applied to Essanay's financial situation as this company went out of existence not long after the film was released. Chaplin's Essanay films, counting *Triple Trouble*, numbered fifteen.

Chaplin began his Mutual films in 1916. He completed twelve films before he left in 1917. Chaplin showed himself at his finest and most original in the Mutual films. Each film had a different theme; each had situations which had never been tried by any of the leading comedy-makers of that time. Chaplin's fertile imagination was envied by those who attempted to imitate his success. When Chaplin left Mutual, the company faded into oblivion; the loss of the great comedian affected Mutual's destiny as it had Essanay's. Chaplin was an important and valuable man.

When Chaplin went to First National, working under a million-dollar contract, he took his time in preparing his films. He made eight films for this company between 1918 and February, 1923, and a film called *The Bond* for the Liberty Loan Committee in 1918 to encourage people to buy bonds for the war effort. Also, in 1918 Chaplin took his first wife, Mildred Harris, a young girl who was having some success in films. She divorced Chaplin in 1920.

Chaplin's best films at First National were *Shoulder Arms*, a comedy gem about an inductee during the first World War, and *The Kid*, a beautifully and imaginatively told story about a tramp who raises an abandoned baby boy. The Kid was portrayed with sympathy and humor by Jackie Coogan under Chaplin's astute direction. Little Jackie was a natural talent and the first figure in a Chaplin film to emerge as an entity unto himself. Jackie Coogan, later active in TV, particularly as Uncle Fester in "The Addams Family," died in 1984 at 69.

The great reception given to *The Kid*, which Chaplin had made as a full-length feature, must have added impetus to his desire to make features exclusively. Chaplin had been contemplating this change to features since 1919, when he had been one of the persons instrumental in the establishment of United Artists as a releasing company for the product of such top stars as Douglas Fairbanks, Sr., and Mary Pickford. He had been unable, however, to release his films through United Artists because of his contract with First National. When Chaplin did join United Artists, he abandoned short comedies forever.

Chaplin's first feature for United Artists did not star him. He wrote *A Woman of Paris* for Edna Purviance, his leading lady since 1915 and a dear friend. Miss Purviance had matured by 1923 and no longer fitted into the mold of a "girl" heroine. Chaplin hoped that this film would be the beginning of a new career for her. Critics praised Chaplin's direction and the film, but found fault with Miss Purviance's performance. When her career sank, Chaplin kept her under contract for the rest of her life even though he could no longer cast her in his films. She later appeared as an extra in *Monsieur Verdoux* and *Limelight* for old times' sake. Edna Purviance died in 1958.

In 1924, Chaplin married Lita Grey, who bore him two sons, Charles Spencer, Jr., and Sydney. This marriage ended in a stormy and much publicized divorce action in 1927. Both Charles Jr. and Sydney became actors; Charles Jr. died at 42 in 1968, of a blood clot.

Two years before the divorce, in 1925, Chaplin released *The Gold Rush*, which was hailed as a screen masterpiece. He had taken time making it, injecting a mixture of pathos and humor into each situation. In 1928, he released *The Circus* and, although it did not please some film critics as much as *The Gold Rush* had, the public received it warmly.

Chaplin decided to make his next film, *City Lights*, a silent picture. While it was in preparation, he received the news that his mother had died. He had always provided for her as best he could even when he was a child. The first person to benefit from his success had been this frail woman who had endured so many illnesses and misfortunes. Chaplin had her come to the United States in 1921, hoping that she would be happier living in California.

City Lights was released in 1931, a year in which

the silent film was considered part of the past. But Charlie, the Little Tramp, though silent, was still very much of the present. *City Lights* proved to be Chaplin's finest achievement. He was indestructible.

Chaplin released still another silent, *Modern Times,* in 1936. A silent film was an even greater gamble in 1936 than in 1931. But Chaplin decided that the *Little Tramp* character must remain voiceless. The viewing public agreed; the new film was a success. In this take-off on man in the age of automation, Chaplin cast Paulette Goddard, whom he had married, as his leading lady. Miss Goddard, a vivacious and intelligent woman, established herself as an actress in other films even before she played the heroine in Chaplin's next film, *The Great Dictator.* Their marriage, however, ended in divorce. Because she, too, now has a home in Switzerland, Charles Chaplin, Jr., once asked her if she ever sees his father. "We live on different mountains," she replied.

Only traces of the Little Tramp can be found in the Jewish barber of *The Great Dictator,* Chaplin's first film with dialogue. The Little Tramp and sound, Chaplin felt, could not exist side by side. Chaplin ridiculed Hitler and his gang as well as Mussolini in this movie, which began his "message" film period. (*Modern Times* did not have enough purposeful elements in it to be considered as such.)

Chaplin's two portrayals as the dictator and the little barber were sketched and acted with perfection. Also, for the first time since *The Kid,* another actor in a Chaplin film gave an equally strong performance. This was Jack Oakie whose Napaloni (or Mussolini) was a first-rate portrayal. Although some critics found flaws in *The Great Dictator,* they still praised Chaplin for his biting attack on totalitarianism and its leaders.

When the United States entered the war against the Axis powers, Chaplin shared with mankind the hope that the Allies would bring about a speedy victory. His trouble began with a speech in which he urged the opening of a second front in Russia. He continued to make speeches and soon began to incur the wrath of several organizations which felt that Chaplin's political leanings were very far left. Chaplin vehemently denied that he was affiliated with any ism, but the damage had been done. To complicate matters, a young woman named Joan Barry brought a paternity suit against him. Blood tests proved that Chaplin could not have been the father of the child in question, but a court trial exhausted his strength and left him embittered.

Chaplin had married Oona O'Neill, daughter of playwright Eugene O'Neill, in 1943, the year in which he was planning his film *Monsieur Verdoux.* When it was released in 1947, Chaplin's popularity was at an all-time low. It seems almost unbelievable that America's favorite clown had become one of the most unpopular figures in films. Chaplin had designed *Monsieur Verdoux* as an antiwar film, but his statements about war and war profiteers came so late in the film that the Verdoux character aroused no sympathy in the audience. Film critics, who recognized and appreciated what Chaplin was trying to put forth, felt the same way. Also, Chaplin was considered a villain by many people, and audiences could not sympathize with a villain portraying a villain.

Today, *Monsieur Verdoux* is looked at in a different light, as is Chaplin himself. Despite its inconsistencies, it is an important film and, for the third time, allowed another performer in a Chaplin film a share of glory. This was Martha Raye, whose interpretation of Annabella is a classic caricature of a noisily shrewd, clumsily passionate, indestructible woman. Chaplin acted wisely in casting Miss Raye in this role; his scenes with her are the most humorous in the film.

Chaplin's last film made in the United States was *Limelight.* It was exhibited in New York in 1952 and officially released in 1953, but it was not shown in many parts of the United States. Resentment against Chaplin was still strong. The majority of New York critics were pleased with the film, which was a story of youth taking over from age. Yet it was more. It was Chaplin saying his farewell to the United States. In 1952, he and Oona left for England, taking with them their four children, Geraldine, Michael, Josephine, and Victoria. Chaplin later settled with his family in Switzerland.

In 1957, Chaplin made *A King in New York* at the Shepperton Studios in England. It has been described as an attack on the United States by some and as a mere satire on the United States by others. Whatever it is, it is clear that Chaplin was speaking of a period in the history of this country which ended some time ago.

Chaplin settled in Switzerland, where his wife, Oona, presented him with four more children, Eugene, Jane, Annette, and Christopher. The eldest daughter, Geraldine, emerged as one of the more interesting actresses in films.

At the beginning of 1966, Chaplin started production on his last film project after an absence of ten years. For the first and only time, he would be working with established stars whose careers he did not further—Marlon Brando and Sophia Loren. He would be working in color and would be producing under the auspices of a major company with which he had no association, Universal Pictures. Pinewood Studios near London housed the production of *A Countess From Hong Kong* and Chaplin entertainingly showed his stars how he wanted them to play his antique farce, which he had first conceived in 1931. Both stars had been so in awe of Chaplin that they agreed to make the film without looking at a script beforehand. Chaplin cast his son Sydney in a major role and gave himself a bit (one of the funniest in the film), with daughters Geraldine, Josephine and Victoria in brief parts.

The premiere was held just one year later in London for a glittering crowd led by the Royal Family's Princess Alexandra of Kent. The critics had gotten their first look at the film only that day and they termed it a flop. Critics, and audiences, were as unkind all over the globe. Brando and Loren wound up not talking to each other during the filming and Chaplin had to remind them they were working in a romantic comedy. The blame, however, was placed directly on Chaplin's shoulders. Characteristically, he termed the critics idiots and defended his film, insisting that the public would side with him. Chaplin.let the people decide. Instead of a bitter ending, he felt that he would reap the benefits of much greater acclaim in just a few years.

In 1971, Classic Festival Corporation—later Classic Entertainment—released a package of Chaplin classics to theatres. The films included *City Lights, Modern Times, The Great Dictator, Monsieur Verdoux, Limelight* (first time in a regular albeit specialized release), *The Chaplin Review* (consisting of *A Dog's Life, Shoulder Arms* and *The Pilgrim*) and *A King In New York,* in its American premiere. In a complicated tangle of corporations, this package passed through several hands as such principals as Mo Rothman, and Howard Goldfarb (HG Entertainment) acquired or disposed of the films. Chaplin's Roy Export Company, founded in Liechtenstein, also licensed the sale of 16mm. prints to the home market.

After a twenty-year exile for political and personal reasons, Chaplin returned to America despite having vowed never to see it again. In April, 1972, he was honored at the "Salute to Chaplin" ceremony in New York City's Lincoln Center and he was awarded a special Oscar at the Academy Award ceremonies in Hollywood. The honorary award was presented to "Charles Chaplin, for the incalculable effect he has had in making motion pictures the art form it is in this century." Following a film clip tribute and a four-minute standing ovation, a deeply moved Chaplin—near tears—could offer only a short speech in which he thanked the "sweet, wonderful people" in the audience. Later, after an equally emotional reunion with Jackie Coogan, a more composed Chaplin admitted that his peers were "like children" in their desire to show their adulation.

This adulation spilled over into the next year. Because it had never played Los Angeles before, the twenty-year-old *Limelight* was finally eligible for Academy Award consideration. It received an Oscar for Best Original Dramatic Score, which Chaplin shared with Raymond Rasch and Larry Russell. On Christmas of 1972, he observed, "All my work was done for myself—done to amuse and to show invention." On August 9, 1974, the still spry Chaplin and wife Oona attended the Switzerland wedding of their fifth child, Eugene, 21, and teacher Sandra Guignard, 20, daughter of a Swiss dentist. Daughter Josephine, who married and divorced Greek furrier Nick Sistovaris, named her son Charlie upon his birth in 1971. She later wed French actor Maurice Ronet.

During his last years, Chaplin periodically announced that he and associate Jerry Epstein would produce *The Freak,* his own screenplay. This was the tale of an angel come to earth in South America. Because of her wings, she is exploited by the London media and the church. Chaplin had written it for Victoria and rehearsed her in the part, but she had left home to marry. Later, he decided to go ahead with filming plans, which never came to be. In 1974, he did bring forth the book *My Life in Pictures,* a photo history of his career with captions that he wrote; he revised it four times in an eight-year period before publication.

When smoking was still in favor, in 1974, Chaplin licensed the manufacture in the U.S. of

Tramps, The Gentle Smoke. Advertised as "buy 'em or bum 'em," they showed Chaplin in his familiar guise on the cover of the pack. In December, 1975, the club Tramps opened in New York City at 125 East 15th Street. Displaying Chaplin stills and artifacts, it came with an intimate Limelight Room. On his 85th birthday, the Lord of Manoir Le Ban, Vevey, Switzerland on Lake Geneva in The Swiss Alps made the observation that motion pictures were "generally better than in the old days." Looking both forward and backward, he said, "The older you get, the more you think of the past, the more you think of death." With a twinkle in his eye, he admitted that he was always very shy, but being rich he could do what he pleased, and being old he could get away with anything. About his career: "I always knew I was a poet."

On March 4, 1975, his native England finally honored one of its most famed sons. Chaplin was knighted, along with 120 Britons, including humorist and fellow expatriate P. G. Wodehouse, 93, and Dr. Roger Bannister, first man to run the four-minute mile. Wearing striped pants, a cutaway, top hat and—in a humorous touch—blue suede shoes, Chaplin sat in a wheelchair as Queen Elizabeth dubbed him Sir Charles, while an orchestra played the theme from *Limelight*. Unable to rise, Chaplin admitted that he was too dumbfounded to speak to the Queen. Later, he did stand for photographers and waived his cane, saying he was going to celebrate by getting drunk and insisting that he not be addressed as Sir Charlie. Due to space restrictions, he was accompanied only by Oona and their two youngest, Annie, 15, and Christopher, 12.

The Queen was also in attendance for Chaplin's next major honor a year later (March, 1976). He was made a fellow of the new British Academy of Film and Television Arts, at London's International Center. Sir Richard Attenborough introduced him as "the greatest man the world of cinema has ever known." A brass mask symbol was presented to Chaplin by the Academy President, Princess Anne. Again, he was in a wheelchair.

Filmic examinations of the master's work were always in vogue. *The Gentleman Tramp* had its premiere at the 1974 Los Angeles International Film Exposition. Chaplin had filmed new scenes for this with Walter Matthau, who also narrated

with Sir Laurence Olivier. Following along the lines of *The Emerging Chaplin* was *Chaplin—A Character is Born* (1977), a 40-minute documentary from S-L Productions, narrated by Keenan Wynn. Beginning with stills from Chaplin's early life and career, this traced his work chronologically and included *Making a Living, Kid Auto Races at Venice, The Tramp, Easy Street, The Vagabond, The Pawnshop, The Rink, The Immigrant* and *The Adventurer*. An earlier compilation was *The Funniest Man In The World* (1967), narrated by Douglas Fairbanks, Jr.

The last project on which Chaplin worked was a new score for *A Woman of Paris* in 1976, for the Bicentennial salute to American Comedy at the Museum of Modern Art in New York. In April, 1978, the film had its first U.S. theatrical release since Chaplin had withdrawn it. Kino International did the honors.

As he had for 25 years, Chaplin attended the Swiss National Circus opening at Vevey in 1976. Late that year, a stroke almost completely incapacitated him. He couldn't walk, stand or feed himself and was barely able to talk. Oona lovingly cared for him, pushing his wheelchair to various places. He watched TV and had his films screened, his favorite being *Monsieur Verdoux*. This productive man, who was fathering children until well into his seventies and was working even in his wheelchair, finally succumbed on Christmas Day, 1977 at 88, in his sleep. On March 1, 1978, grave robbers stole his remains from the Vevey cemetery, but they were recovered sixteen days later, never having left Switzerland.

Interest in his life and work was far from over. The film *The Emerging Chaplin, Vol. II* (1980) was distributed, written and edited by Israel Berman. Among the many books about him were *Chaplin, His Life and Art* (McGraw-Hill, 1985) by David Robinson, film critic of the London *Times*; this was the authorized biography, initiated by Jerry Epstein. Another was called simply *Charlie Chaplin* (Harper & Row, 1985), a pictorial documentary by Maurice Bessy, former director of the Cannes Film Festival, who had known Chaplin in Hollywood. An oddity was *Charlie Chaplin's Own Story* (University of Indiana Press, 1986), edited by Harry M. Geduld. This was in fact actually written by Rose Wilder Lane (1887-1968) and originally published in 1916 by Bobbs-Merrill but withdrawn when Chaplin complained about it. The writer thought that it was a highly complimentary work and couldn't understand why he had objected. Of the more than 500 books in some 37 languages (as of 1980), two of the most definitive remain Theodore Huff's 1951 biography and Chaplin's own *My Autobiography* (The Bodley Head, London, 1964).

In 1981, actor George Hamilton bought the Chaplin estate in Beverly Hills for $1 million from Joy and Lawrence Light, who had lived on the property since 1957, after the government had confiscated it for taxes. Mrs. Light had actually signed her estate over to Hamilton in 1976 for just $400,000. However, he hadn't the money at the time; he later made more money from investments than he ever had for acting. So, they settled the deal for a little over $1 million, even though the estate was worth $3 million. In December, 1987, Christie's auction house in London handled 260 items of Chaplin material. His bowler hat and cane were sold for $154,200, bought by a Dane, Jorten Strecker, for display at his cinema-restaurant in Copenhagen. IBM Computers used a young actress to do an unauthorized but completely appealing portrayal of Chaplin in its TV commercials in this country.

Proof that the government had finally forgiven Chaplin came to light in 1986 when the United States Information Agency extended its free loan of Chaplin films to American embassies. The films were shown as a goodwill gesture and the number of items increased from the previous five to eleven.

Among the Chaplin films which have come to light is a home movie made about 1929, showing the literary giants of the day participating in a spoof of *Camille*, with Chaplin recreating his Dance of The Ocean Rolls from *The Gold Rush*. In November, 1982, the London Film Festival held the long delayed premiere of *How to Make Movies* (1918), a 23-minute short which Chaplin made to mark the opening of his Hollywood studios. His stars Edna Purviance, Eric Campbell and Albert Austin appear with him, playing golf on the backlot. First National thought it unplayable and it was never released. It was resurrected by British film historians Kevin Brownlow and David Gill, who edited the film from Chaplin's original cutting instructions. Carl Davis conducted a 30-piece orchestra, performing his own score, and Chaplin children Jane, Annie and Eugene were in attendance.

Brownlow and Gill are without doubt the leading authorities on Chaplin and the most generous distributors of his lost material. They produced the marvelous Thames Television "Hollywood" series and were looking for a piece of Chaplin film to include. Rachel Ford, Chaplin's longtime business manager, kept his film vaults near London and invited them to look at a scene cut from *City Lights*. This led to the discovery that she had not destroyed any of Chaplin's unused footage, as he had wished. Realizing what was there, they obtained Oona's permission to use the material and the three-part "Unknown Chaplin" resulted. This superb three-part Thames Television presentation was narrated by James Mason in one of his last assignments. Among the gems is *The Professor* (1923), an uncompleted film in which Chaplin plays the owner of a flea circus. It developed that he used the camera to edit his ideas as he improved upon or abandoned them altogether. Other material for the series came from France. Shown in England in 1983, "Unknown Chaplin" didn't reach American TV until 1986.

Chaplin's centennial in 1989 marked merely the first century in the history of this comedy legend.

The COMPLETE FILMS of
CHARLIE CHAPLIN

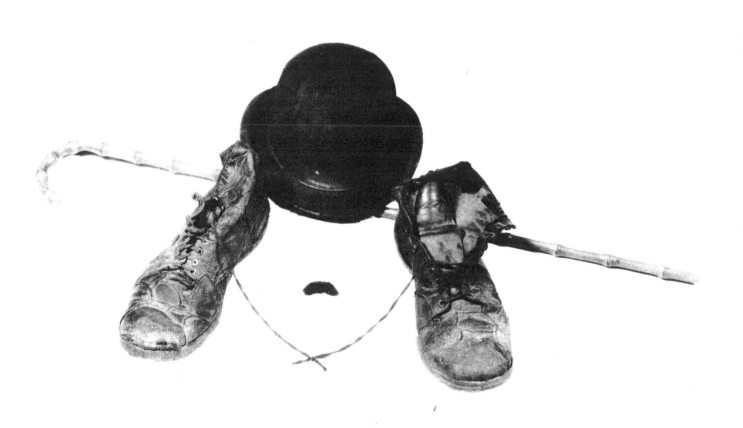

Chaplin in his screen debut as
" the nervy and very nifty sharper."

Making a Living

A Keystone Comedy Released in One Reel (February 2, 1914)

CAST

Charles Chaplin, Chester Conklin, Alice Davenport, Minta Durfee, Virginia Kirtley, Henry Lehrman.

CREDITS

Directed by Henry Lehrman. Photography attributed to E. J. Vallejo.

SYNOPSIS

A sharper (Chaplin), posing as a distinguished lord, introduces himself to a family of some wealth. He makes a good impression on the mother and begins to court the pretty blonde daughter. But the daughter's fiancé, a newspaper photographer from whom the sharper has borrowed money, lets it be known that the pretended lord is a penniless imposter. The sharper decides to earn his living and is engaged as a newspaper reporter. His job depends on getting a certain sensational photograph, so he steals the newspaper photographer's camera containing the negative of this great scoop. A chase follows and the photographer is caught by the police. The sharper succeeds in reaching the newspaper office before his rival, turns in the film, and makes the big scoop.

In his first film, Chaplin appeared in high hat and frock coat, with a monocle and a drooping mustache. He was the Englishman of high fashion somewhat gone to seed. He had worn a similar costume

One way to make a living is to borrow money. (With Henry Lehrman).

Another way: to do your worst but get there first.

on the stage in one of the acts of the Karno Pantomime Company. But to American audiences it seemed much like the garb worn by the villains they had hissed in the old stage melodramas.

What was said about
    MAKING A LIVING
Moving Picture World
    The clever player who takes the role of the nervy

and very nifty sharper in this picture is a comedian of the first water, who acts like one of Nature's own naturals. It is so full of action that it is indescribable, but so much of it is fresh and unexpected fun that a laugh will be going all the time almost. It is foolish-funny stuff that will make even the sober-minded laugh, but people out for an evening's good time will howl.

A memorable moment: The Little Tramp discovers the motion picture camera.

Kid Auto Races at Venice

A Keystone Comedy Released in a Split Reel, the other half being an educational short, Olives and Their Oil *(February 7, 1914)*

CAST

Charles Chaplin, Charlotte Fitzpatrick, Gordon Griffith, Billy Jacobs, Henry Lehrman, Thelma Salter.

CREDITS

Directed by Henry Lehrman. Photography by Frank Williams, who was to be the cameraman for almost all the Chaplin films made by Keystone.

SYNOPSIS

When a cameraman attempts to film a kiddy-car contest, Charlie, a stranger from Who Knows Where, makes his appearance. Comic and camera-happy, he laughs with the children, mimics them, and flies into rages which soon pass. He begins his long battle with the police, whose defense of order arouses his eternal protest. Wherever the

Charlie, front and center, steals the scene.

A posed shot of Chaplin, with Henry Lehrman and Frank D. Williams, cameraman.

frustrated cameraman turns, Charlie is there—in the camera's eye—stealing the scene. The spectators are content to be roped off from the fun, but Charlie is a free spirit and moves to the center of things as his natural right.

The film was made on the boardwalk at Venice, California, where a real auto race for children was being held. The action was quite impromptu and the filming, it is said, was done in about forty-five minutes. For his second picture Chaplin had miraculously found the costume he was to wear, with few exceptions, for more than thirty years. His film character was also born then, but audiences and Chaplin, too, were to spend years learning more and more about the wandering and wondering little fellow.

What was said about
KID AUTO RACES AT VENICE

Bioscope

Some sensational happenings are witnessed during the contests between the baby cars, while the funny man persistently obstructs the eager camera men in their operations.

The Cinema

Kid Auto Races struck us as about the funniest film we have ever seen. When we subsequently saw Chaplin in more ambitious efforts our opinion that the Keystone Company had made the capture of their career was strengthened. Chaplin is a born screen comedian; he does things we have never seen done on the screen before.

Mabel Normand, the finest comedienne of the silent screen, played with Chaplin in eleven Keystone comedies.

Mabel's Strange Predicament

A Keystone Comedy Released in One Reel (February 9, 1914)

CAST
Charles Chaplin, Chester Conklin, Alice Daven-port, Harry McCoy, Hank Mann, Mabel Normand, Al St. John.

CREDITS
Directed by Mack Sennett and Henry Lehrman.

A quiet night in Hotel Keystone. Left to right: Harry McCoy, Hank Mann, Chaplin, Alice Davenport, and Mabel Normand.

SYNOPSIS

Charlie has had one drink too many when he enters a hotel. In the lobby he tries to make a call on a pay phone but he does not have a nickel. Mabel, with her dog on a leash, appears. Charlie, soon hopelessly entangled in the leash, falls to the floor and gets his hand caught in a spittoon. But he manages to maintain the utmost dignity. Mabel has become a magnet to him and in this comedy of errors, ending in disaster, he pursues her relentlessly. Later, when Mabel is in her pajamas, she tosses a ball to her pet collie. The ball rolls into the hallway, and when she runs out to get it the door to her room closes and locks. Then she sees Charlie in the hallway. She darts into the nearest room and hides under the bed where she is discovered by a very jealous wife.

What was said about
MABEL'S STRANGE PREDICAMENT

Exhibitors' Mail

The Keystone Company never made a better contract than when they signed on Chas. Chaplin, the Karno performer. It is not every variety artiste who possesses the ability to act for the camera. Chaplin not only shows that talent; he shows it in a degree which raises him at once to the status of a star performer. We do not often indulge in prophecy, but we do not think we are taking a great risk in prophesying that in six months Chaplin will rank as one of the most popular screen comedians in the world. Certainly there has never been before quite so successful a first appearance.

In this early version of the tramp costume, Charlie did not wear his famous shoes.

Emma Clifton, Chaplin, Ford Sterling, and Chester Conklin.

Between Showers

A Keystone Comedy Released in One Reel (February 28, 1914)

CAST

Charles Chaplin, Chester Conklin, Emma Clifton, Ford Sterling.

CREDITS

Directed by Henry Lehrman.

SYNOPSIS

Charlie and Ford Sterling are in Westlake Park.

It has been raining and they struggle for possession of an umbrella in this comedy of "two fatuous adorers and their efforts at gallantry." A young lady has come upon the scene and they contend with guile and fury for the right to assist her across a puddle of water.

Chaplin's screen characterization, as it was to be seen in the later Keystone comedies, was almost fully developed in this film. Henry "Pathé" Lehrman, Chaplin's first director, left Keystone for L-Ko after *Between Showers* was completed.

What was said about
BETWEEN SHOWERS

The Cinema

A screamingly funny comedy, featuring Charles Chaplin and a charming girl. All the trouble is caused by an umbrella, and the two men's rivalry for the favour of the lady. Their efforts to out-do each other in gallantry create many humorous situations.

Kinematograph Weekly

We feel we are doing a good turn to our exhibitor readers in advising them to secure all the Chaplin releases they can get a booking for. We have seen seven Chaplin releases, and every one of them has been a triumph for the one-time hero of "Mum-ming Birds" [a favorite Karno pantomime] who has leapt into the front rank of film comedians at a bound. Chaplin has created an entirely new variety of screen comedian—a weird figure in whom one may recognise elements of the dude, the tramp, the acrobat, and, flavouring all, the "silly ass" of whom the drunken swell in "Mumming Birds" was so perfect a type. This extraordinary character wanders through the recent Keystone releases—there is no other word to describe the Chaplin touch—and indulges in escapades which are side-splitting in their weird absurdity and their amazing suddenness. Chaplin has more than made good and those who wish to see him at his best should put a mark against *Mabel's Strange Predicament, Kid Auto Races,* [and] *Between Showers.*

The "fatuous adorers" come to a showdown.

Mack Sennett, who developed slapstick comedy into one of the "Seven Lively Arts," started Chaplin on his career as a movie actor.

A Film Johnnie

A Keystone Comedy Released in One Reel (March 2, 1914)

CAST

Charles Chaplin, Roscoe ("Fatty") Arbuckle, Minta Durfee, Virginia Kirtley.

CREDITS

Made under Mack Sennett's supervision.

SYNOPSIS

Charlie, in a nickelodeon, is charmed by the pretty girl he sees on the screen. He goes to the Keystone Studio to find her. He wrecks several sets, then follows the film-makers to a real fire. A rescue scene is staged and filmed, but Charlie ruins the negative.

This was the first of the films in which Chaplin

The old Keystone studio at Edendale, California.

Movie-struck Charlie meets a film star, Fatty Arbuckle.

used a film studio as the scene of action. Wonderful records of the early studios are also found in *The Masquerader, His New Job,* and *Behind the Screen.*

What was said about
   A FILM JOHNNIE

Moving Picture World
   Edgar English's [Chaplin's!] work in this picture will keep it amusing.

Bioscope
   Another triumph for the old Karno comedian. Knockabout of an extraordinary character. An extra special comedy.

The Cinema
   The sensation of the year is the success of Chas. Chaplin, whom trade reviewers declare far funnier in Keystones than even in "Mumming Birds." One of his films is *A Film Johnny* which shows how his admiration of a film beauty led to a commotion in a cinema and finally took him to the Keystone Studio—and a job. All the Keystone heads are in this and it is packed with indescribably funny incidents.

[34]

Ford Sterling, Keystone's first star comedian, played without make-up in TANGO TANGLES.

Tango Tangles

A Keystone Comedy Released in One Reel (March 9, 1914)

CAST

Charles Chaplin, Roscoe ("Fatty") Arbuckle, Chester Conklin, Ford Sterling.

CREDITS

Made under Mack Sennett's supervision.

SYNOPSIS

Charlie, without costume or make-up, goes to a public ballroom which is crowded with dancers in fancy costumes. The dance craze was then at its height in America and Charlie does not know what to make of it. Fatty is there and the bandleader takes a great fancy to Fatty's girl. But both men are enraged because she persistently dances with Charlie. The impromptu shenanigans end in a glorious free-for-all fight.

Chester Conklin, Chaplin's partner in many Keystone escapades.

Mack Sennett later said, "We took Chaplin, Sterling, Arbuckle, and Conklin to a dance hall, turned them loose, and pointed a camera at them. They made like funny, and that was it." Chaplin had been hired by Keystone to take the place of Ford Sterling, who had given notice that he was leaving the company. Sterling's specialties were villains, "Dutch" comics, and in a class by itself, the Chief of the Keystone cops. This was Sterling's last appearance with Chaplin. His departure accounts for the fact that in so many of the Keystone films Chaplin's role was essentially that of a villain.

What was said about
TANGO TANGLES

Bioscope
Jealousy in a dance room ends in a fight which is engaged in by the dancers, musicians and attendants.

The Cinema
The ball-room is soon converted into a battlefield, which results in this Keystone being a real scream!

His Favorite Pastime

A Keystone Comedy Released in One Reel (March 16, 1914)

CAST

Charles Chaplin, Roscoe ("Fatty") Arbuckle, Peggy Pearce (also known as Viola Barry).

Charlie as the amorous bar-fly.

Fatty Arbuckle, who played the husband in HIS FAVORITE PASTIME.

CREDITS
Directed by George Nichols.

SYNOPSIS

Charlie actually has two pastimes, tipping the bottle and flirting with the girls. While doing a little serious drinking in a saloon he succeeds in making life miserable for the other customers. He then meets a girl, follows her home, and soon encounters a highly outraged husband.

In France this one was called *Charlot entre le Bar et l'Amour.*

What was said about
  HIS FAVORITE PASTIME

Moving Picture World

The comedian, whose favorite pastime is drinking cocktails, is clever, in fact, the best one Mack Sennett has sprung on the public. He is a new one and deserves mention.

Motion Picture News

If there is an audience anywhere that does not roar when they see this comedy they cannot be in the full possession of their wits. It is absolutely the funniest thing the Keystone Company has ever put out, and this is not written by a press agent. Mr. Chaplin has introduced a number of funny actions that are original to the American stage.

Syracuse Post-Standard

The producer of a Charlie Chaplin film doesn't have to go abroad in search of color and atmosphere. For that matter, the piece of limburger cheese which shares the honors with Charlie in *His Favorite Pastime* provides an atmosphere of its own. Charlie's India rubber countenance does the rest. In the final scene we see him at the top of a telegraph pole while an enemy below is busy with an axe. Charlie lowers the limburger at the end of a string. This drives away the enemy. A typical Chaplin piece. Also typical of moving picture humor. Anything less obvious will hardly go over in the films.

Minta Durfee, first wife of Fatty Arbuckle, played in CRUEL, CRUEL LOVE.

Chester "Walrus" Conklin encouraged Chaplin to remain in the movies at a moment when he was ready to quit.

Cruel, Cruel Love

A Keystone Comedy Released in One Reel (March 26, 1914)

CAST
   Charles Chaplin, Chester Conklin, Alice Davenport, Minta Durfee.

CREDITS
   Made under the supervision of Mack Sennett.

SYNOPSIS
   Lord Helpus (Chaplin), having been caught flirting with the maid, is jilted by his sweetheart. He decides to end it all by taking poison, but the butler changes the potion. Lord Helpus then receives a note of forgiveness from his sweetheart, but he thinks it has come too late. Doctors are summoned and after an examination announce that our hero will live. The poison was merely a harmless glass of water.

   It can never be assumed that a film has completely disappeared, but there is no record of a surviving print of *Cruel, Cruel Love* or of three other Chaplin films, *Mabel's Strange Predicament, A Busy Day,* and *Her Friend the Bandit.* Of the films which have become quite rare, more of them can be found in France than in the United States.

What was said about
   CRUEL, CRUEL LOVE

Moving Picture World
   Slight in texture, but it makes a pleasing, laughable picture.

Young Edgar Kennedy, who became master of the "slow burn."

The Star Boarder

A Keystone Comedy Released in One Reel (April 4, 1914)

CAST

Charles Chaplin, Alice Davenport, Gordon Griffith, Edgar Kennedy.

CREDITS

Made under the supervision of Mack Sennett.

SYNOPSIS

Charlie, in his boardinghouse, is a great favorite with the proprietor's wife. All the male boarders dislike him, however, and arrange to frighten him with a dummy. Charlie *is* frightened and runs for the police. A tramp, meanwhile, has hidden himself in a cupboard, the police find him, and Charlie

has the last laugh. The film also introduces a magic-lantern show. The son of the boardinghouse keepers has taken a set of compromising pictures and shows them to the assembled guests. They all see Charlie kiss the proprietor's wife; then, to even the score, they see the proprietor flirting with a charming lady.

What was said about
THE STAR BOARDER

Motion Picture News

A very funny comedy. The landlady is too familiar with the star boarder to suit her husband. He gets even, however, by going out with another woman.

A motorcycle spin which was soon followed by a spill. (With Mabel Normand.)

Mabel at the Wheel

A Keystone Comedy Released in Two Reels (April 18, 1914)

CAST

Charles Chaplin, Chester Conklin, Harry Mc-Coy, Mabel Normand, Al St. John, Bill Seiter, Mack Sennett.

CREDITS

Directed by Mack Sennett and Mabel Normand.

SYNOPSIS

Charlie is on a motorcycle, with Mabel sitting behind him. She falls off into the mud and he drives on. The story, tied to the Vanderbilt Cup Race, then moves to the drivers who are competing, and to the wild car race that takes place. While her lover, Harry, is held captive by Charlie's henchmen, Mabel takes his place at the wheel. Charlie has watered the track and all the cars skid, turn, and start racing in the opposite direction. But Mabel wins the race.

Chaplin's natural inventiveness had been held down by his directors, the self-centered Henry Lehrman and the conservative George Nichols. He felt more at ease working directly under Mack Sennett, who was receptive to his suggestions. When the twenty-year-old Mabel Normand took over the direction of *Mabel at the Wheel,* telling him what he could and could not do, Chaplin broke out in open rebellion. He was ready to quit,

Mabel's racing car hero (Harry McCoy).

Harry McCoy and Mabel Normand, with Charlie as the villainous sportsman.

but Mack Sennett stepped in as peacemaker and co-director, Chaplin apologized to Mabel Normand, and Miss Normand began to seek Chaplin's advice.

What was said about
MABEL AT THE WHEEL

New York Dramatic Mirror

The bright particular star who carries the male lead is Charles Chaplin. Long acquaintance with the speaking stage, and a naturally funny manner of appearing, have made him, in the three months' experience that he has had in motion pictures, second to none. Mabel Normand carries the female lead with her usual bright success. This is a Keystone comedy, having said which you proceed to qualify by all the adjectives standing for funny, burlesque, grotesque, farcical or screaming that you can think of, and leave with the fear that you have not done it justice. Yes, there is no sense in it, as usual.

Twenty Minutes of Love

A Keystone Comedy Released in One Reel (April 20, 1914)

CAST

Charles Chaplin, Chester Conklin, Minta Durfee, Gordon Griffith, Edgar Kennedy, Joseph Swickard.

CREDITS

Made under the supervision of Mack Sennett.

Since Chaplin used the same plot for the Essanay comedy In the Park, *he presumably provided the story for this earlier version.*

SYNOPSIS

Charlie, strolling in the park, finds that love, as in the song, is "busting out all over." He happily joins two lovers on a bench, but is eventually made to realize that if two make a couple, three make a

Love is in bloom in Westlake Park. (Gordon Griffith, Minta Durfee, and Edgar Kennedy.)

Charlie gets a girl.

crowd. On another bench a girl is left alone while her boyfriend steals a watch to give her as a present. Charlie steals the watch from him and gives it to the girl. The boy friend returns and Charlie, the persistent but unsuccessful suitor, is in trouble. But he is again in possession of the watch and he tries to sell it to the man from whom it was originally stolen. In the final chase, Charlie manages to push everyone into the lake except the girl. Love is still in the air and they walk off together.

The complications of this lively charade are best summarized in a title under which it was later distributed, *Cops and Watches.*

What was said about
TWENTY MINUTES OF LOVE

Kinematograph Weekly
Plenty of the comic element is introduced and the person who does not laugh at the peculiar antics of Chas. Chaplin—well, must be hard to please.

Bioscope
Here Chaplin plays the part of the undesired but persistent suitor. The comic element is given special prominence and is quite safe in the hands of this well-known comedian.

The romantic life of the Premier of Greenland. (With Mabel Normand.)

Caught in a Cabaret

A Keystone Comedy Released in Two Reels (April 27, 1914)

CAST

Charles Chaplin, Phyllis Allen, Chester Conklin, Alice Davenport, Minta Durfee, Gordon Griffith, Alice Howell, Edgar Kennedy, Harry McCoy, Wallace MacDonald, Hank Mann, Mabel Normand, Mack Swain, Joseph Swickard.

CREDITS

Directed by Mabel Normand and Charles Chaplin. Written by Chaplin and advertised as "Produced by Miss Normand."

SYNOPSIS

Charlie, billed as "The Ham-and-½," is a waiter in a cheap cabaret, where his special duty is to hammer obnoxious customers over the head. He is given an hour off and takes his dog for a walk. He meets Mabel, saves her from a robber, and then gives her his card. It reads "The Premier of Greenland." Later he attends Mabel's party and makes a hit as the "Premier." Like Cinderella, however, he must leave before the party ends to resume his work at the cabaret. The girl's lover is jealous of Charlie and plans to expose him. He suggests a slumming party and they all go to the cabaret, where they discover that Charlie is a waiter. A good old Keystone riot, complete with pie-throwing, takes place, with Mabel scoring a knockout when she catches Charlie.

This is the first film in which Chaplin is known

The real life of the cabaret waiter.

to have had some share in the direction. It was done with great informality, Mabel Normand supervising Chaplin's scenes, Chaplin "directing" Mabel, and all the actors and crew making whatever suggestions occurred to them.

What was said about
CAUGHT IN A CABARET

New York Dramatic Mirror

Superlatives are dangerous epithets, especially when dealing with pictures. For that reason it is unwise to call this the funniest picture that has ever been produced, but it comes mighty close to it.

Bioscope

Mr. Charles Chaplin and Miss Mabel Normand are seen at their best in this two-reel farce. The cabaret waiter, during his evening out, rescues a lovely damsel, and, posing as a foreign potentate, makes a great impression, until the lady and her friends happen to visit the cabaret at which he is employed. Mr. Chaplin has a humour all his own, in which here he has the opportunity of indulging to the utmost, the result being amusing in the extreme.

Moving Picture World

This is another two-reel comedy manufactured in Mack Sennett's comical factory out in Californy State. It caused so much laughter you couldn't hear what the actors was talkin'. Charles Chaplin was the leading fun maker.

Mack "Ambrose" Swain, perennially the deceived husband.

Caught in the Rain

A Keystone Comedy Released in One Reel (May 4, 1914)

CAST
Charles Chaplin, Alice Davenport, Alice Howell, Mack Swain.

CREDITS
Written and directed by Charles Chaplin.

SYNOPSIS

Charlie, in one of his hotel comedies, flirts with a married lady and gets into trouble with her husband. Later, in his hotel, the same lady walks in her sleep and enters Charlie's room. The husband comes into the room and discovers his wife. Charlie's innocent explanation is not accepted by the irate husband. He knocks Charlie out the window —and the rain falls on our fallen hero.

Chaplin, with four months' experience in films, was now recognized by the Keystone staff and his fellow players as a master comedy-maker. In this film he was not only an actor, but also author, director, and gagman. It was not one of the best of his Keystone comedies but it was the first film for which he was completely responsible. He was later to draw upon some of its ideas and incidents when he was making his Essanay comedies.

What was said about
CAUGHT IN THE RAIN

Bioscope
Chaplin flirts with a married lady and gets into much trouble. The climax comes when he takes part in a comical sleep-walking scene at the hotel. His explanations cause a riotous finale.

Charlie as the jealous wife.

A Busy Day

A Keystone Comedy Released as a Split Reel, the other half being an educational short, The Morning Papers *(May 7, 1914)*

CAST
  Charles Chaplin, Mack Swain.

CREDITS
  Written and directed by Charles Chaplin.

SYNOPSIS
  Charlie, in one of Alice Davenport's dresses, gives his first female impersonation. He is the jealous wife who attends a harbor festival and surprises "her" husband when he is making love to a pretty girl. Mad as a wet hen, Charlie gets into a tangle with the police and ends in the water. In the background of this short film, said to have been made in two hours, are views of San Pedro harbor and some interesting glimpses of American navy ships.

What was said about
  A BUSY DAY

Bioscope
  [Chaplin] gives an amazing exhibition of acrobatic humour.

Ambrose (Mack Swain) is caught with another woman.

Ambrose receives his punishment.

Mabel Normand as the disdainful heroine.

The two experts with bricks and mallets (Mack Sennett and Chaplin.)

The Fatal Mallet

A Keystone Comedy Released in One Reel (June 1, 1914)

CAST

Charles Chaplin, Mabel Normand, Mack Sennett, Mack Swain.

CREDITS

Reputedly directed by Chaplin, Mabel Normand, and Mack Sennett.

SYNOPSIS

Charlie and Mack Sennett are rivals over Mabel and struggle violently to have precedence in courting her. But the disdainful Mabel is hard to please. A swift kick in her rear, delivered with precision by Charlie, at least gains the lady's attention. She may seem to prefer Mack, but this only increases Charlie's determination to win her.

Iris Barry, viewing the film years after it was made, found it charming. "It was quite exquisitely silly," she wrote in *Let's Go to the Movies.* "People stood behind a barn door and hit each man who entered on the head with a chunk of wood. It was like a game of nine-pins in which the nine-pins themselves took part."

What was said about
THE FATAL MALLET

Bioscope

Though rivals in love for the beautiful Mabel Normand, Charles Chaplin and Mack Sennett combine to rid themselves of a third poacher on their preserves, and the employment of a deadly mallet gives these indescribable comedians the opportunity for another genuinely funny farce.

Moving Picture World

This one-reeler proves that hitting people over the head with bricks and mallets can sometimes be made amusing.

Her Friend the Bandit

A Keystone Comedy Released in One Reel (June 4, 1914)

CAST

Charles Chaplin, Charles Murray, Mabel Normand.

CREDITS

Directed by Charles Chaplin and Mabel Normand.

SYNOPSIS

Charlie is an elegant bandit with whom Mabel has a flirtation. Mabel has a party and Charlie, after a neat display of banditry, comes to it posing as a French nobleman. In high society, however, Charlie is not so elegant and his behavior shocks Mabel's guests. But the Keystone cops move in and move Charlie out.

Echoes of this old comedy turned up in two of Chaplin's later films, *The Count* and *The Adventurer*.

What was said about
HER FRIEND THE BANDIT

Moving Picture World

Charles Chaplain [sic] and Charles Murray play the chief funny characters of this farce which is a bit thin; but it has the rough whirling of happenings usually found in farces of this well-marked type.

Bioscope

Mr. De Beans [the Count] is captured by the bandit in question while on his way to a reception given by Mrs. De Rocks. The bandit assumes Mr. De Bean's evening suit and invitation card and, being a Keystone reception, he is taken on credit and has a gay time until the Keystone police are called in, who, it is needless to say, liven things up considerably and put the climax to an arousing farce.

Charlie Murray, one of the best of the Keystone comics, who plays the role of Count De Beans.

The fight begins. (Mack Swain, Fatty Arbuckle, Al St. John, Chaplin, and Edgar Kennedy.)

The Knockout

A Keystone Comedy Released in Two Reels (June 11, 1914)

CAST

Charles Chaplin, Roscoe ("Fatty") Arbuckle, Joe Bordeaux, Charles Chase, Edward Cline, Minta Durfee, Alice Howell, Edgar Kennedy, Hank Mann, Al St. John, Mack Sennett, Slim Summerville, Mack Swain.

CREDITS

Made under the supervision of Mack Sennett.

SYNOPSIS

Charlie appears rather briefly in the second reel of this Fatty Arbuckle comedy. Fatty is a heavyweight boxer and fights Ed Kennedy. When his skill in the manly art of self-defense fails, Fatty resorts to a revolver. Charlie is the troublemaking referee who sees that Fatty gets more than his share of punches. The comic prize fight ends in a frenzied chase with those officers of law and lunacy, the Keystone cops.

Edgar Kennedy, Arbuckle's opponent in this film, could really fight—he once did fourteen rounds with Jack Dempsey. Fatty was supported in the film, as he so frequently was, by his wife, Minta Durfee, and his nephew, Al ("Fuzzy") St. John, known to a later generation of moviegoers as the bearded comic in many Western films.

What was said about
THE KNOCKOUT

Moving Picture World
Roscoe Arbuckle, ably supported, makes barrels of fun in this two-reel comedy release. In its early stages, the story has a particularly well-connected plot, but things go to smash a little in this line when a big chase is introduced in the second reel. This chase, as well as a comedy prize fight, is unusually funny.

The referee is the first to fall. (Mack Swain, Chaplin, Fatty Arbuckle, and Edgar Kennedy.)

Mabel Normand as the hot dog vendor.

Mabel's Busy Day

A Keystone Comedy Released in One Reel (June 13, 1914)

CREDITS

Directed by Charles Chaplin and Mabel Normand.

CAST

Charles Chaplin, Billie Bennett, Chester Conklin, Harry McCoy, Wallace MacDonald, Mabel Normand, Slim Summerville.

SYNOPSIS

Charlie, with a flower in his lapel and a stiff drink under his belt, finds Mabel selling hot dogs

Charlie investigates the financial situation of Miss Billie Bennett.

Charlie consoles the
ruined businesswoman.

at the race track. Although she is supposedly pro-
tected by a doting police sergeant, Charlie is hungry. He stops a man from stealing one of the hot
dogs, then proceeds to steal one for himself, and
then another. A chase follows, the hot dogs are
grabbed by the bystanders, and Mabel's business
is seemingly ruined. Charlie then turns on his
charm and consoles the angry girl.

What was said about
    MABEL'S BUSY DAY

Moving Picture World
    In this comedy the usual strenuous work of the
Keystone artists, headed by Mabel Normand and
Charles Chaplin, almost makes the screen on which
it is thrown visibly wobble.

Motion Picture News
    Any comedy with Charles Chaplin and Mabel
Normand the leads is sure to be an immense success. There is no plot at all, but the events that
transpire in the one reel are side-splitting.

Bioscope
    The business in question consists of selling sau-
sages on the racecourse, and . . . it may be imagined
that pretty Mabel's business is strenuous and mirth-
provoking. The fun never flags, and is well up to
the Keystone average.

Charlie with the real prizefighter (Mack Swain).

Charlie with the dummy.

Mabel's Married Life

A Keystone Comedy Released in One Reel (June 20, 1914)

CAST

Charles Chaplin, Alice Davenport, Alice Howell, Wallace MacDonald, Harry McCoy, Charles Murray, Mabel Normand, Mack Swain.

CREDITS

Directed by Charles Chaplin and Mabel Normand.

SYNOPSIS

Charlie leaves his wife, Mabel, because he is jealous of her attentions to a prize fighter. Mabel, on the other hand, is angry because Charlie did not knock the fighter down. Charlie goes to a bar and gets so plastered he forgets he has determined to end his marriage. Full of courage supplied to him over the counter he returns home, where he is confronted by a boxing dummy which Mabel has placed in the doorway, hoping it will make a fighter out of him. Charlie fights his best, but the dummy wins.

What was said about
MABEL'S MARRIED LIFE

Motion Picture News

All will be aching from laughter when it is over.

Bioscope

The mixup between Mabel, Charles and the dummy is extremely funny, and in the restaurant Mr. Chaplin gives a very excellent study in inebriation. This is certainly one of the best of the Keystone comedies.

Moving Picture World

Charles Chapman [sic] and Mabel Normand are at their best, and everyone knows what that means.

Laughing Gas

A Keystone Comedy Released in One Reel (July 9, 1914)

CAST

Charles Chaplin, Alice Howell, Fritz Schade, Slim Summerville, Joseph Sutherland, Mack Swain, Joseph Swickard.

CREDITS

Written and directed by Charles Chaplin.

SYNOPSIS

Charlie works for Dr. Pain, the dentist. He enters the waiting room with great dignity, bows to the patients as if he were Dr. Pain himself, then picks up the cuspidor and departs. He quarrels with the dentist's other assistant, then accosts the dentist's wife, causing her to lose her skirt. While Dr. Pain comforts his wife, Charlie feels called upon to take care of the patients. He chooses a pretty girl, seats her in the dentist's chair, then holds her nose with the forceps while he kisses her. When the dentist returns, the battle begins.

What was said about
LAUGHING GAS

Motion Picture News

Besides getting into a fight with two of his master's patients and getting generally in the way, he [Chaplin] doesn't do anything except create roars of laughter.

Bioscope

Mr. Charles Chaplin appears as a dentist's assistant, and works with enormous energy in his own peculiar way. This is an uproarious farce of a kind which is likely to create unrestrained mirth for its particular class of audience.

Charlie treats Mack Swain to one of his famous kicks.

Charlie, as the would-be dentist, administers a mallet on Joseph Swickard.

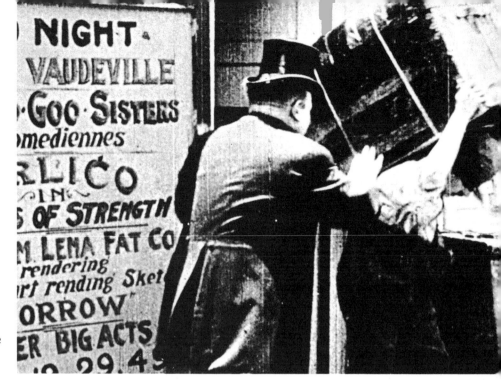

Charlie carries in the wardrobe trunk.

The Property Man

Touching "the homely strings of our own vulgarity."

The prop man props up the dancer.

A Keystone Comedy Released in Two Reels (August 1, 1914)

CAST

Charles Chaplin, Charles Bennett, Harry McCoy (in a bit part), Lee Morris, Fritz Schade, Mack Sennett (in a bit part).

CREDITS

Written and directed by Charles Chaplin.

SYNOPSIS

Charlie is a prop boy and Jack-of-all-trades behind the scenes in a small music hall. Trouble begins with the performers in the handling of their luggage and the assignment of their dressing rooms. Trouble continues at the rehearsal and reaches heights of confusion in the actual performance, when all the acts get mixed with each other. Charlie had earlier made an old man do most of his heavy work, but he obligingly "helps" the strong man in his act by briskly carrying off the fake weights he has been lifting before an impressed audience. At the end, Charlie settles an argument with a fire hose, turning it on the washed-out performers and the audience.

What was said about
THE PROPERTY MAN

Moving Picture World

There are very few people who don't like these Keystones. They are thoroughly vulgar and touch the homely strings of our own vulgarity . . . they are not the best pictures for a parlor entertainment, this is true. There is some brutality in this picture and we can't help feeling that this is reprehensible. What human being can see an old man kicked in the face and count it fun?

Bioscope

There are so many uproariously absurd situations in this Chaplin comic, all consequent upon the ardent desire of our friend "Props" to run the whole of the affairs "behind" that the vaudeville entertainment becomes one long chapter of unrehearsed happenings, much to the delight of an audience of which comical Mack Sennett forms a distinguished member.

"Did you ever see a woman for whom your soul you'd give,
With a form like the Milo Venus, too beautiful to live?"
(With Cecile Arnold and Vivian Edwards.)

The Face
on the Barroom Floor

A Keystone Comedy Released in One Reel (August 10, 1914)

CAST

   Charles Chaplin, Cecile Arnold, Chester Conklin, Vivian Edwards, Fritz Schade.

CREDITS

   Directed by Charles Chaplin. Based on the poem of the same title.

SYNOPSIS

   Charlie burlesques the poem about the skid-row bum who had been a famous artist before his wife deserted him, running off with another man. Charlie drifts into a saloon—" 'Twas a balmy summer's evening and a goodly crowd was there"—is given a drink, and tells his story. In one of the flashbacks he sees his wife as he chanced to meet her later, with the man she no longer loves and with her four obstreperous children. This is a comforting memory, but he continues to weep and tell his sad tale in order to get another drink. In the midst of a brawl he begins to draw on the floor. However, it is not "the face that might buy the soul of any man" but a series of circles and crosses.

   The subtitles of the film were lines from the poem, but the original verses were altered to match the Keystone credo that life is a funny game at best.

What was said about
   THE FACE ON THE BARROOM FLOOR

Moving Picture World
   Chas. Chaplain [sic] wins new laurels in the leading part.

Charlie does some serious reading.

The fine art of throwing a brick.

Recreation

A Keystone Comedy Released in a Split Reel, together with a travel short, The Yosemite *(August 13, 1914)*

CAST
Charles Chaplin.

CREDITS
Written and directed by Charles Chaplin.

SYNOPSIS
Charlie, seated in a park, gives his expert attention to the picture of a girl on the cover of the *Police Gazette.* He hasn't a real girl and becomes so depressed over the fact that he prepares to drown himself. He changes his mind, however, when a girl approaches. It soon turns out that she has a sailor friend. When he comes up the two men fight. Soon two cops are brought into a brick-throwing battle filled with retreats, diversionary movements, and surprise attacks. Charlie has opportunities to renew his ardent flirtation and eventually settles matters by pushing the cops and the sailor into the lake.

The violence in this little film is performed with such grace and rhythm that it seems to become a ballet of bricks and brawling. In attempting to list a cast for the film, various writers have suggested such players as Chester Conklin, Mabel Normand, Alice Davenport, and Rhea Mitchell. None of these, nor any of the identifiable "name" actors of Keystone, was among the four other players who made up the cast.

What was said about
RECREATION

Bioscope
[Chaplin's adventures] pack a short film with an abundance of his peculiar humor. This quaint actor is here seen in one of his most typical parts.

The Cinema
Our gallant hero . . . gets into trouble with the police, and then the fun begins, fast and furious, but Charlie has a peculiar manner entirely his own, and the way he tries to extricate himself from an awkward position is very whimsical, but unfortunately for himself, he is not quite successful.

Charlie, masquerading as a
woman, enchants the director
(Charlie Murray).

The Masquerader

*A Keystone Comedy Released in One Reel (August
27, 1914)*

CAST

*Charles Chaplin, Roscoe ("Fatty") Arbuckle,
Cecile Arnold, Charles Chase, Chester Conklin,
Minta Durfee, Vivian Edwards, Harry McCoy,
Charles Murray, Fritz Schade.*

CREDITS

Written and directed by Charles Chaplin.

SYNOPSIS

Charlie is a movie actor and is introduced without costume or make-up. He is at the studio and
gets into his familiar garb to go before the camera.
But he pays attention to the girls and not to the
director. He misses his cue, spoils the scene, gets
into the wrong set, and is finally fired. He then
dresses as a woman and returns to the studio. He
so charms the director that he is hired as a leading
lady. The actors are turned out of their dressing
room so that the new "actress" may have it. Charlie
then gets back into his usual costume. When his
imposture is discovered he is again fired and chased
from the studio.

What was said about
THE MASQUERADER

Bioscope

Here we have Mr. Chaplin rehearsing for a cine-
matograph production, in which he gives a really
remarkable female impersonation. The make-up is
no less successful than the characterisation, and is
further proof of Mr. Chaplin's undoubted versatility.

Charlie is himself enchanted and seems
to fly to heaven. (With Vivian Edwards
and Cecile Arnold.)

Trouble on the boardwalk.

His New Profession

A Keystone Comedy Released in One Reel (August 31, 1914)

CAST

Charles Chaplin, Charles Chase, Minta Durfee, Harry McCoy.

CREDITS

Written and directed by Charles Chaplin.

SYNOPSIS

Charlie is hired to wheel an invalid around the park. He begins his work with enthusiasm, but he soon thinks he should be earning a little extra, so he puts a beggar's sign on the old man. A pretty girl, a beggar, and the old man's nephew, who is furious because Charlie has almost let the old man in his wheel chair fall into the water, see to it that Charlie's "new profession" is soon a thing of the past.

What was said about
HIS NEW PROFESSION

Motion Picture News

Charlie Chaplin appears in this picture and as usual, whenever he appears it is a laugh throughout. .

Mr. Full and Mr. Fuller at the cabaret.
(Fatty Arbuckle and Chaplin.)

The Rounders

A Keystone Comedy Released in One Reel (September 7, 1914)

CAST

Charles Chaplin, Phyllis Allen, Roscoe ("Fatty") Arbuckle, Charles Chase, Minta Durfee, Wallace MacDonald, Al St. John, Fritz Schade.

CREDITS

Written and directed by Charles Chaplin.

SYNOPSIS

Charlie and Fatty, as Mr. Full and Mr. Fuller, are roisterers who are out on a glorious drunk. Returning home, each of them is given a bad time by his wife. While the wives wrangle, the men collect all the money they can find in the house and slip out again. They go to a restaurant where the wives later find them, happily disgracing themselves. At the end, they are in a boat on the lake, sleeping peacefully as the boat slowly sinks.

Chaplin and Arbuckle made a remarkable team in this film. Arbuckle admired Chaplin and some years later paid this tribute to his co-star: "I have always regretted not having been his partner in a longer film than these one-reelers we made so rapidly. He is a complete comic genius, undoubtedly the only one of our time and he will be the only one who will be still talked about a century from now."

What was said about
THE ROUNDERS

Moving Picture World

It is a rough picture for rough people, that people, whether rough or gentle, will probably have to laugh over while it is on the screen . . . Chas. Chapman [*sic*] and the Fat Boy appear in this as a couple of genial jags.

The prodigal's return. (With Phyllis Allen.)

The tipplers end up in the Big Drink.

The janitor falls in love with the secretary (Minta Durfee).

The New Janitor

A Keystone Comedy Released in One Reel (September 24, 1914)

CAST

    Charles Chaplin, Jack Dillon, Minta Durfee, Al St. John, Fritz Schade.

CREDITS

    Written and directed by Charles Chaplin.

SYNOPSIS

    Charlie becomes a janitor, but is soon fired as a "blundering boob" when he drops a pail of water, which falls on his boss standing below in the street. While in the act of leaving his lost job he hears the stenographer ring for help. He returns, saves that distressed beauty, and catches the robber who has broken into the company's safe.

    In this story of humor and suspense, so similar to *The Bank* which Chaplin made later, the expected moment of disillusionment never comes. The film has importance in the development of the Chaplin screen character because Chaplin discovered while making it that he could make people feel sorry for him.

What was said about
THE NEW JANITOR

Bioscope

    Charles Chaplin for once appears as a successful hero, for while employed as an office-cleaner, though he shows little aptitude for his work, he happens to rescue the typist from assault and secure a burglar who is robbing the office safe. Mr. Chaplin's eccentric methods are as entertaining as ever.

Moving Picture World

    A ripping good comedy number, with Chas. Chapman [*sic*] playing the part of the janitor. He interpolates a lot of his inimitable funny business and the plot is better than usual.

Motion Picture News

    The comical Charles Chapman [*sic*] in a laughable farce that will arouse peals of laughter from any audience.

Charlie stops the robber with his pistol.

Straightening up by stepping over his hands, he still has the robber covered.

One of the girls Charlie loves and loses (Cecile Arnold, who later changed her name to Cecile Arley).

Those Love Pangs

A Keystone Comedy Released in One Reel (October 10, 1914)

CAST

Charles Chaplin, Cecile Arnold, Chester Conklin, Vivian Edwards, Edgar Kennedy, Harry McCoy, Norma Nichols.

CREDITS

Written and directed by Charles Chaplin.

SYNOPSIS

Charlie, intent upon getting a girl, finds that other gentlemen resent his attempts to steal their sweethearts. He tries to make time with his landlady, but she favors Chester. He then has an unsuccessful flirtation in the park. Discouraged, he attempts to drown himself but is rescued. Finally he goes to a nickelodeon and succeeds in winning the interest of two fair charmers. When he falls asleep the girls slip away and his rivals find him. They wreck the movie house and toss the unhappy lover through the screen.

What was said about
   THOSE LOVE PANGS

Moving Picture World
   Charles Chaplin and Chester Conklin disport themselves in further love affairs in this number.

Bioscope
   The volatile Charles succeeds in making himself agreeable to two ladies at a picture show, but his rivals succeed as usual in reducing him to a state of mental and physical collapse.

Charlie mans the oven.

Dough and Dynamite

A Keystone Comedy Released in Two Reels (October 26, 1914)

CAST

Charles Chaplin, Phyllis Allen, Cecile Arnold, Charles Chase, Chester Conklin, Vivian Edwards, Edgar Kennedy, Wallace MacDonald, Norma Nichols, Fritz Schade, Slim Summerville.

CREDITS

Directed by Charles Chaplin. Based on ideas supplied by Chaplin and Mack Sennett, with Sennett registered as author in the copyright entry.

SYNOPSIS

Charlie and Chester are waiters, but when the employees of the adjoining bakery go on strike they are sent to man the ovens. They, and the rest of the cast, wallow in dough before the bakery is demolished by dynamite which the strikers have concealed in a loaf of bread. At the picture's end, Charlie is buried in dough. Then his head slowly emerges; our hero is himself again.

Originally planned as a scene for *Those Love Pangs*, the opportunities for high jinks in a bakery grew until it became a separate two-reel comedy, one of the most famous of all of Chaplin's Keystones.

What was said about
DOUGH AND DYNAMITE

New York Dramatic Mirror

In a comparatively short time Charles Chaplin has earned a reputation as a slapstick comedian, second to none. His odd little tricks of manner and his refusal to do the most simple things in an ordinary way are essential features of his method, which thus far has defied successful imitation.

Moving Picture World

Two reels of pure nonsense, some of which is very laughable indeed. Chas. Chaplin appears as a waiter in a French restaurant and bakery. He has a terrible time breaking dishes and getting the

Charlie brings in the freshly baked bread.

dough over the floor. The bakers go on a strike and at the last the whole place is blown up by dynamite. This is well-pictured and very successful for this form of humor.

Motion Picture News. Reviewed by Peter Milne.

When Charles Chaplin, the inimitable English comedian, is supported by a star, hardly less renowned, Chester Conklin, it is a safe bet that one may settle back in his seat to indulge in continuous laughter, for he will see a slapstick comedy of the highest order . . . And if by chance he sees the name of Chaplin outside of any theatre in the future he will most surely enter, for the simple reason that he knows that Chaplin is funny at all times.

A fair visitor comes to the kitchen (Norma Nichols).

Charlie at the auto races.

Gentlemen of Nerve

A Keystone Comedy Released in One Reel (October 29, 1914)

CAST

Charles Chaplin, Phyllis Allen, Charles Chase, Chester Conklin, Alice Davenport, Mabel Normand, Slim Summerville, Mack Swain.

CREDITS

Written and directed by Charles Chaplin.

SYNOPSIS

Charlie has a day at the auto races. He hasn't any money to pay for his admission but gets in through a hole in the fence. Chester has brought Mabel to the races, but they have a quarrel. Consequently, Charlie gets to sit with Mabel and has free refreshments by drinking pop from a bottle held by an inattentive girl. When Chester is arrested by the cops, Charlie and Mabel really begin to enjoy the races.

What was said about
GENTLEMEN OF NERVE

Moving Picture World

Chaplin, Conklin and Mabel appear in this interesting bit of nonsense . . . and perform a lot of funny antics of an eccentric sort.

Bioscope

Charles Chaplin as the very "broke" gentleman who is anxious to make love to all the pretty girls assembled to watch some daring motor-races, manages to obtain an abundance of humour out of every situation. It is just the type of film that audiences have grown to appreciate with great gusto.

Motion Picture News

Charlie, Chester and Mabel attend an auto race. Results? As laughable as ever were pictured.

Mabel with her penniless admirers
(Chaplin and Mack Swain).

Charlie's donkey is not a music lover.

Charlie, the piano mover, is fortified with a drink. With Charles Chase (far right).

His Musical Career

A Keystone Comedy Released in One Reel (November 7, 1914)

CAST

Charles Chaplin, Phyllis Allen, Joe Bordeaux, Charles Chase, Alice Howell, Fritz Schade, Mack Swain.

CREDITS

Written and directed by Charles Chaplin.

SYNOPSIS

Charlie, with Ambrose as his helper, is a piano-mover. He has been assigned to deliver a piano to one address and to remove one from another address where the would-be purchaser has defaulted in his payments. But Charlie gets this mixed up. He delivers the piano, not to Mr. Rich, the millionaire for whom it is intended, but to the bad debtor. He then begins to remove a piano from the millionaire's home. When this is vigorously protested, he and Ambrose give it a push down the street and into the lake. But Charlie is in front of the piano and he, too, is forced down the hill. Before he and the piano sink into the water, Charlie has time to play a few last lost chords.

Some of the situations in *His Musical Career* remind us of one of Laurel and Hardy's masterpieces, made many years later—*The Music Box.*

What was said about
HIS MUSICAL CAREER

Bioscope

A screaming farce in which Mr. Charles Chaplin, assisted by a donkey, is quite at his best . . . *Mabel at the Wheel* and *His Musical Career* are further examples of the skill with which the individual characteristics of these two popular favourites, Miss Normand and Mr. Chaplin, are presented in a fresh and original form. Miss Normand's thrilling motor race . . . and his hefty deeds as a piano shifter, will compare favourably with any of their previous achievements, and induce the hope that they are the forerunners of many more successes from the joint efforts of Mr. Mack Sennett and his inimitable comedians.

Variety

One of the best short comedies in a month. Funny piano moving skit.

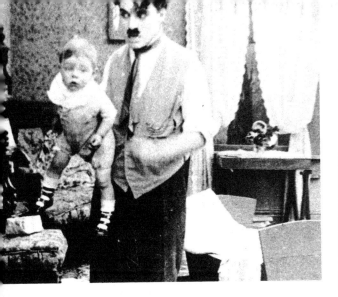

Charlie minds the baby.

His Trysting Place

A Keystone Comedy Released in Two Reels (November 9, 1914)

CAST

Charles Chaplin, Phyllis Allen, Mabel Normand, Mack Swain.

CREDITS

Written and directed by Charles Chaplin.

SYNOPSIS

Charlie is the husband who is forced to acknowledge that his wife, Mabel, is boss. Ambrose too is henpecked. Meeting in a restaurant, the two men quarrel and each gets into the other's coat by mistake. Charlie's wife finds a note from a girl in the coat Charlie is wearing and drives him from the house. In the park he comes upon Ambrose's wife. She has found a bottle in Ambrose's coat. They commiserate with each other on the miseries of marriage. Mabel discovers them together and the sparks fly. When peace is at last restored, Charlie hands Mrs. Ambrose the love note that was found in Ambrose's coat pocket.

[73]

Mabel Normand delivers
a parting salute.

The happy ending.

What was said about
HIS TRYSTING PLACE

Montgomery Journal. Reviewed by Louis Reeves Harrison.

The comic spirit is entirely too deep and subtle for me to define. It defies analysis. The human aspect is certainly dominant. It is funniest when it is rich in defects of character. The incongruity of Chaplin's portrayals, his extreme seriousness, his sober attention to trivialities, his constant errors and as constant resentment of what happens to him, all this has to be seen to be enjoyed. He merely sits down in the kitchen to read the war news, while Mabel tries to tend baby on the kitchen table and make bread at the same time. He leans back and puts one foot on the stove, upsetting the boiling kettle, when a flame leaps up and burns his leg, then trouble begins.

Moving Picture World

Chaplin does some particularly amusing stunts in this and the fun runs high through the entire two reels.

The leading players in the first feature-length film farce: Chaplin, Marie Dressler, Mabel Normand.

Tillie's Punctured Romance

A Keystone Feature Released in Six Reels (November 14, 1914)

CAST

Charles Chaplin, Marie Dressler, Mabel Normand, Phyllis Allen, Billie Bennett, Charles Bennett (who played the rich uncle and two minor characters), Joe Bordeaux, Charles Chase, Chester Conklin, Alice Davenport, Minta Durfee, Alice Howell, Gordon Griffith, Edgar Kennedy, G. G. Ligon, Harry McCoy, Wallace MacDonald, Charles Murray, Mack Swain, with Al St. John, Slim Summerville, Eddie Sutherland, and Hank Mann as Keystone cops.

The parson sees that heaven protects the working girl.

A quiet and sleepy evening
with the idle rich.

CREDITS

Directed by Mack Sennett. Adapted by Hampton Del Ruth from Tillie's Nightmare, *a musical comedy with book and lyrics by Edgar Smith, music by A. Baldwin Sloane.*

SYNOPSIS

Charlie is a city slicker who gets Tillie (Marie Dressler) to steal her father's savings and run away with him. After they reach the city he takes her money and returns to Mabel, his former sweetheart and partner in crime. The country maiden, deserted and now destitute, gets a job in a restaurant. When Charlie learns that her uncle has died and left her a great fortune, he hastily decides to wive it wealthily by proposing marriage. Tillie first learns that she is an heiress after the wedding, and she then realizes why Charlie has married her. But she forgives him and they make the grand entrance into her inherited mansion. They decide to celebrate by giving a ball. They dance a memorable tango, but Tillie is soon on a rampage. Mabel is there as a maidservant and is discovered by Tillie while she is being kissed by Charlie. It now turns out that the rich uncle is *not* dead. He returns when Tillie, after having thrown pies and wildly shot her revolver, is trying to strangle Charlie. The uncle's appearance gives Charlie an opportunity to escape with Mabel. Tillie follows and soon the uncle and the Keystone cops are in mad pursuit. On the pier the cops push Tillie into the water and they all come tumbling in after her. When she is finally fished out she lets Charlie know that their romance is over. Mabel also spurns Charlie and he is left alone whik the two women agree that "He ain't no good to neither of us."

Tillie's jealousy is observed by
a party guest (Billie Bennett).

This was the first successful feature comedy and remains one of the most famous films of the early days. It was actually made in the spring of 1914. It was finally released in November after months spent in working out the best possible method of distribution for a big picture which could not be made to fit into the regular Keystone program. It was a personal triumph for Chaplin and made him a star of the first magnitude.

What was said about
TILLIE'S PUNCTURED ROMANCE

Moving Picture World. Reviewed by George Blaisdell.

Charles Chaplin plays opposite Miss Dressler . . . Chaplin outdoes Chaplin; that's all there is to it. His marvelous right-footed skid—and it seems to make no difference whether he has under him rough highway or parlor floor—is just as funny in the last reel as it is in the first . . . When Mack Sennett was in the East a couple of months ago he confided to a friend that in the making of his six-reel comedy in which Miss Dressler was starred, he had given all that he had. After viewing *Tillie's Punctured Romance* we are bound to say he had a lot to give.

Motography. Reviewed by Charles R. Condon.

Up to the present time multiple reel comedies of three reels or more have been more or less experiments, and, in the majority of cases, absolute failures as far as preserving purely comedy situations and atmosphere is concerned . . . In view of the tremendous success which the New York Motion Picture Corporation has made of its six-reel Keystone comedy, *Tillie's Punctured Romance*, it marks an epoch in this most popular department of photoplay. It is the "Cabiria" of comedy. Genuine humor is the dominating note in every scene.

Variety

Tillie's Punctured Romance came from the title role Miss Dressler played in *Tillie's Nightmare*. She is splendidly supported by the Keystone Company, including Charles Chaplin, Mabel Normand, Mack Sennett, Mack Swain and others. Miss Dressler is the central figure, but Chaplin's camera antics are an essential feature in putting the picture over. Mack Sennett directed the picture and right well has he done the job.

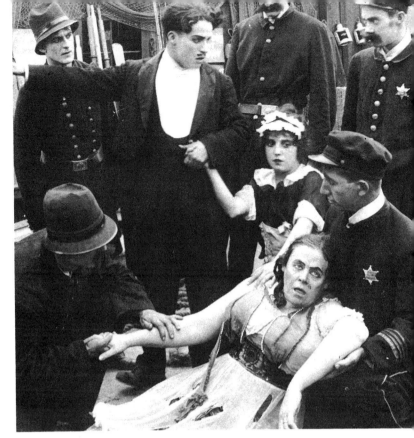

Tillie is rescued from the sea by the Keystone Cops.

Tillie renounces Charlie.

Charlie's wife and Mabel's husband find their spouses holding hands. (Phyllis Allen, Mabel Normand, Chaplin, and Mack Swain.)

Getting Acquainted

A Keystone Comedy Released in One Reel (December 5, 1914)

CAST

Charles Chaplin, Phyllis Allen, Cecile Arnold, Edgar Kennedy, Harry McCoy, Mabel Normand, Mack Swain.

CREDITS

Written and directed by Charles Chaplin.

SYNOPSIS

Charlie is back in the park, where he is chaperoned by his formidable wife, Mrs. Sniffles. Mabel is also in the park with husband Ambrose. Charlie is attracted to Mabel while the jealous Ambrose is attracted to Mrs. Sniffles. It is "A Fair Exchange,"

as the film was later called, until a policeman who is unsympathetic to flirtations in the park breaks up the newly acquainted couples. Charlie is arrested, but his wife comes to the rescue and takes her naughty husband home.

What was said about
GETTING ACQUAINTED

Moving Picture World

Mabel Normand, Charles Chaplin and the others are undeniably comical in this lively farce.

The Cinema

Yet another fine Charles Chaplin number, including the celebrated Mabel Normand.

Charlie dreams of the prehistoric past.

His Prehistoric Past

A Keystone Comedy Released in Two Reels (December 7, 1914)

CAST
  Charles Chaplin, Cecile Arnold, Gene Marsh, Al St. John, Fritz Schade, Mack Swain.

CREDITS
  Written and directed by Charles Chaplin.

SYNOPSIS
  Charlie makes a journey into time. Falling asleep on a park bench, he dreams of the prehistoric past. In an ancient kingdom he is Weakchin, clad in bearskin and derby, who flirts with the ruler's favorite. Weakchin and the ruler, Lord Lowbrow, become great friends until Weakchin's pursuit of the favorite makes trouble. Weakchin throws the ruler over a cliff and reigns in his stead. But Lord Lowbrow was not killed by his fall and he is rescued by his fool. He returns to wreak vengeance upon the usurper of his throne. He beats Weakchin over the head—and Charlie wakes up to find a policeman clubbing him and asking him to move on.

At the court of Lord Lowbrow. (Chaplin, Al St. John, and Mack Swain.)

Surrounded by the beauties of a prehistoric harem.

The king is dead (or soon will be). Long live the king!

His Prehistoric Past was the last of Chaplin's Keystone films. He had made thirty-five comedies during his year with Mack Sennett and had earned a little less than ten thousand dollars. In this final film, with the names of the characters reminiscent of those in D. W. Griffith's film of a prehistoric age, *Man's Genesis,* Chaplin introduced the dream followed by the disillusioned awakening. He was to dream again in *The Bank, Shoulder Arms, Sunnyside, The Kid,* and *The Idle Class,* only to return to reality and to some degree of misery.

What was said about
HIS PREHISTORIC PAST

San Francisco Call and Post

Charles Chaplin and other members of the Keystone Company have outdone all their previous fun-provoking efforts in the two-part film called *His Prehistoric Past,* which puts Chaplin in a "dream" state during which time he goes through a series of prehistoric difficulties trying enough to discourage even the strongest "stone age" man.

The rude awakening from the dream of ancient times.

Charlie asks the studio manager for a job.

His New Job

An Essanay Comedy Released in Two Reels (February 1, 1915)

CAST

Charles Chaplin, Agnes Ayres (an extra), Frank J. Coleman, Charles Insley, Charlotte Mineau, Gloria Swanson (an extra), Ben Turpin, Leo White.

CREDITS

Written and directed by Charles Chaplin. Camera work by R. H. Totheroh.

SYNOPSIS

Charlie goes to a film studio, the Lockstone, to get a job. He has a pleasant flirtation with a young girl in the waiting room. He finally gets to see the manager, walking over the prostrate body of another applicant (Ben Turpin), who tried to get to the door first. Charlie does not get hired, but he wanders through the studio and is spotted by a director. He is mistaken for a property man and put to work. The studio becomes a disaster area when Charlie brings in a piece of upright scenery.

"A King's Ransom" is being filmed and the leading man has not arrived. Charlie is asked to rehearse his part. In a uniform too large, with a tremendous shako on his head and an unmanageable sword at his side, he blunders through his role as a romantic hero. He kisses the hem of the train of his leading lady with such prolonged feeling that he does not realize, nor does she, that he is holding her skirt in his hands while she has moved majestically to the top of the stairs. When the leading man arrives, Charlie is fired. The embattled studio, after a mad chase, will never finish "A King's Ransom."

Chaplin's first film for Essanay was made in the Chicago studio and presents a fascinating but highly satirical glimpse of movie-making. Working without a formal scenario, much of the film's fun was impromptu. A playful jibe at Keystone was made obvious by calling the studio the "Lockstone." The photography for the film was done by Rollie Totheroh, then at the beginning of his forty-year association with Chaplin.

The comedians who worked with Chaplin at

Charlie with Ben Turpin. The manner in which Charlie gets into the movies is similar to the actual way Turpin, a janitor-office boy at Essanay, became a movie comedian.

Keystone were later to sing his praises. Ford Sterling, Al St. John, Charlie Chase, Mabel Normand, and Chester Conklin, in recalling the old days, spoke of him with profound respect. And Mack Sennett was to say, "Charlie Chaplin is the greatest of all the artists who worked for me. So you know how much I regretted losing him." At Essanay Chaplin was first teamed with Ben Turpin and on the screen they made a wonderful pair. But Ben, alone among famous comedians, disliked Chaplin and considered him a snob. Chaplin was too exacting in his direction; he was reaching for something Ben was never to understand. Chaplin often exasperated him with his orders to "Do this, do not do that, look that way, walk like this, now do it over." In telling of his grievances some years later to Robert Florey (who described Turpin as a foul-mouthed vulgarian), Ben added, "Besides, I have since proved that I could work without him. I am now the star of Keystone, and my films make lots of money."

What was said about
HIS NEW JOB

Chicago Tribune

It is absolutely necessary to laugh at Chaplin in ten-ninths of his antics in his disaster-attended search for a new job—the small point in which is evidenced the only irony in the picture.

Bioscope

There is probably no film comedian in the world more popular with the average picture theatre

The new actor meets his leading lady (Charlotte Mineau).

Charlie becomes a movie star. Agnes Ayres, who later became a star, is the girl in black lace at Charlie's right.

audience than that famous funmaker, Charles Chaplin, whose services have recently been secured by the Essanay Company. The art of Charles Chaplin defies analysis, and disarms the critic. Just *why* he is so funny, it is almost impossible to say, and very probably he could not tell you himself. He possesses a naturally comic personality and its humour is accentuated by the originality of the innumerable bits of "business," with which his work is so profoundly interspersed. Scarcely a moment passes while he is on the screen, but he is up to some wild piece of mischief or committing some ludicrous folly. And perhaps the funniest thing of all is his own complete imperturbability. Whilst those all around him are rolling in an agony of mirth at his extravagant blunders, he himself pursues his course unmoved, with an air of mild detachment and stolid indifference. Good humorists never laugh at their own jokes. They realise the value of apparent seriousness. And, in the same way, Charles Chaplin remains emotionless, and even absent-minded, in the very midst of his maddest escapades.

The fall of the brave hero. (Ben Turpin sitting on the pillar, with Charlie underneath.)

Gloria Swanson, at the beginning of her remarkable career, was seen briefly in HIS NEW JOB.

Edna Purviance, the beautiful girl from Paradise Valley,
who was Chaplin's leading lady from 1915 to 1923.

A Night Out

An Essanay Comedy Released in Two Reels (February 15, 1915)

CAST

Charles Chaplin, Fred Goodwins, Bud Jamison,
Edna Purviance, Ben Turpin, Leo White.

CREDITS

Written and directed by Charles Chaplin.
Camera work by R. H. Totheroh.

Testing the limits of a stupendous thirst.
(Ben Turpin, Chaplin, and Leo White.)

SYNOPSIS

Charlie and Ben have been trying to drink the town dry. When Charlie returns to his hotel he is not sober enough to know where he is. He goes up to the desk, tries to put his foot on a phantom brass rail and drink the ink. When he finally gets to his room it is still early evening, but he prepares for bed. He solves the problem of hanging up his coat, which has continually fallen to the floor, by absentmindedly thrusting it through the window. It falls to the sidewalk below. Across the hall a dog seizes the slipper of a young married lady (Edna Purviance) and runs with it into Charlie's room. Then comes the charming young wife in her pajamas, pursuing the dog. Both the dog and Edna hide under Charlie's bed. The husband tries to find Edna and while he is downstairs she slips back into her room. But Charlie follows her, gets into bed, and promptly goes to sleep. He is discovered by the husband and is chased. Ben finds Charlie on the street and they go from one café to another.

The irate husband turns out to be the headwaiter at one of them. Charlie throws a custard pie at a Frenchman, washes in the fountain, and is thrown out. Again at the hotel, Charlie knocks at the door of the young wife. Her husband opens the door. Under his threatening stare Charlie retreats to his own room, packs his suitcase, and realizing that escape is the better part of valor, leaves the hotel.

A Night Out was made at the Essanay Studio in Niles, California, although some of the scenes were shot in Oakland. Chaplin drew upon some of the material used in *Mabel's Strange Predicament* for the hotel sequences. In prints of the film as now shown, re-edited with a musical sound track, the sequence of events seems to have been altered.

Edna Purviance was introduced to the screen in *A Night Out*. Born in Paradise Valley, Nevada, she was then nineteen years of age. Work on *A Night Out* had been held up because a suitable leading lady had not been found. When a young

Charlie finds how the decanter works.

cowboy actor said he had frequently seen a very pretty girl in a San Francisco restaurant, Chaplin immediately arranged for an interview. The old fan magazines used to tell the story, although it probably was not true, that four hours later Edna Purviance was standing before a motion-picture camera for the first time in her life. This beautiful actress proved to be amazingly adaptable. Whether she played a waif, a woman of wealth, a country girl, or a most alluring Carmen, she was the perfect leading lady for Chaplin, often providing a center of tranquility in a world of comic madness. She played in every film he made from 1915 through 1923, except in the womanless *One A. M.* and *His New Job.*

What was said about
A NIGHT OUT

Bioscope

Chaplin goes out with his friend, Ben Turpin, for an evening's entertainment, and the fun is cer-

Charlie and Ben (with the discomfited Leo White) consider the shortest distance to the next saloon.

Charlie helps Ben unlock the door.

tainly fast and furious. The sight of these two disreputable tramps mixing with the company in a gorgeous restaurant and behaving in a manner which would not be tolerated in an East-end bar-house, is sufficiently amusing in itself, and by disregarding any pretense at realism adds to the absurdity and enjoyment of a humour that is extravagant to the last degree. Chaplin appears in the old familiar costume, and does all the old familiar business, some of which might well be spared, but most of which is rendered even funnier by its constant repetition. The ease and apparent lack of effort with which Chaplin works his quaint tricks show him to be a very conscientious and hard-working actor in his own peculiar line.

The Cinema

The hero [Chaplin] is magnificently and consistently drunk from first to last. Accompanied by his knock-about partner, Ben Turpin, he sets out to test the limits of a stupendous thirst. . . . This film gives Chaplin full elbow-room for many extraordinary antics and touches of humorous detail, and the fun runs along at top speed. There is little or no actual plot, Charlie having very wisely been given his head, and we should imagine that, at the finish of the production, it was a very sore head. Turpin makes an excellent partner, and takes many a stunning knock-out blow with paralytic indifference.

Charlie and a lady's pocketbook.

The two gentle companions who have to fight
if they are to eat.

The Champion

An Essanay Comedy Released in Two Reels
(March 11, 1915)

CAST

Charles Chaplin, Lloyd Bacon, Bud Jamison,
Edna Purviance, Leo White, with G. M. Anderson
("Broncho Billy") appearing briefly as an extra.

CREDITS

Written and directed by Charles Chaplin.
Camera work by R. H. Totheroh.

SYNOPSIS

Charlie and his faithful bulldog have found a
frankfurter. Charlie is very hungry, but the dog
must have the first bite. The dog, however, refuses
to touch it until Charlie sprinkles some salt on it.
Charlie then passes the training quarters of Spike
Dugan, the champion prize fighter, and learns that
sparring partners are wanted. He picks up a horseshoe for good luck and, strictly from hunger,
applies for a job. After seeing three assailants carried out unconscious, Charlie realizes that the best
place for the horseshoe is in one of his boxing
gloves. With his "lucky" gloves Charlie twice
knocks down the champion, who runs from the
gym begging for mercy. Charlie is now the golden
boy and is scheduled for a championship bout.
While he is training a gambler tries to get him to
throw the fight. But Charlie is certain he will lose
anyway as he has learned that horseshoes are not
allowed. On the night of the big fight Charlie,
billed as the "Jersey Mosquito," has reached the
fourth round and is taking a beating. His dog
watches the fight, smiles when Charlie scores, becomes fierce, then gloomy, when Charlie is knocked

Charlie gets strong encouragement to throw the fight. (Chaplin, Leo White.)

down. The dog finally enters the ring and belabors the antagonist while Charlie scores a knockout and then receives homage as the new champion.

Spike, the dog who gave such a wonderful performance in *The Champion*, was killed by an automobile a few weeks after the completion of the picture. G. M. Anderson, who made a guest appearance, was the first star of Western films and had made his motion picture debut in the famous Edison film of 1903, *The Great Train Robbery*. He was one of the two founders of the Essanay Company. It was from the initial letter of the last names of George K. Spoor and Anderson that the name of the company was created.

What was said about
   THE CHAMPION

New York Dramatic Mirror
   A two-part comedy featuring Charles Chaplin and including what is without doubt the funniest burlesque prize fight ever shown upon the screen.

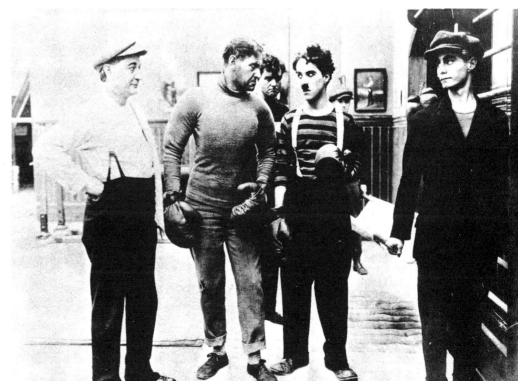

Two men are ready with the stretcher when Charlie meets the prizéfighter.

Charlie filches the hot dogs.

In the Park

An Essanay Comedy Released in One Reel (March 18, 1915)

CAST

   Charles Chaplin, Lloyd Bacon, Bud Jamison, Edna Purviance, Leo White.

CREDITS

   Written and directed by Charles Chaplin. Camera work by R. H. Totheroh.

SYNOPSIS

   It is spring, and Charlie's fancy turns to thoughts of love. But a thief comes out of the bushes and furtively slips his hand in Charlie's pocket. He finds it empty, but meanwhile Charlie's hand has gone into the thief's pocket, first bringing out a cigarette and then a match. Charlie lights up, tips his hat to the thief and thanks him. He sees an ardent Frenchman with his sweetheart, then a nursemaid with her swain. Charlie gets a lesson in love from the Frenchman and decides to try his technique on the nursemaid. He passes a hot-dog stand and with the aid of his cane steals six or seven hot dogs. He then flirts with the nursemaid but she is angered and calls her portly cavalier. Mean-while the thief has discovered the Frenchman and his girl and has stolen her pocketbook. He sees Charlie's hot dogs and while he tries to steal them Charlie retrieves the stolen pocketbook. He sells it to the nursemaid's beau, buys it back again, gives it to the thief, steals it back from him, and finally presents it to the nursemaid. Later he finds the Frenchman trying to commit suicide because his girl has jilted him because of the pocketbook. He hesitates, but Charlie, at his most obliging, holds his watch and money, then kicks him in the water. All the others who are pursuing Charlie get pushed into the water too. Charlie's springtime fancy then turns to the pretty nursemaid—and to the pocketbook he gave her.

What was said about
   IN THE PARK

Bioscope
   The one and only Charlie is seen to the best advantage in this riotous farce which is as wildly funny as it is absurd. Unlike many comedians, Chaplin is always amusing. There seem to be no grey patches in his work. It is all one long scarlet scream.

The introduction of the bogus count. (Paddy McGuire, Chaplin, Lloyd Bacon, Edna Purviance, and Fred Goodwins.)

A Jitney Elopement

An Essanay Comedy Released in Two Reels (April 1, 1915)

CAST

Charles Chaplin, Lloyd Bacon, Fred Goodwins, Paddy McGuire, Edna Purviance, Leo White.

CREDITS

Written and directed by Charles Chaplin. Camera work by R. H. Totheroh.

SYNOPSIS

Charlie, poor and hungry, is waiting for something to turn up. The beautiful Edna appears on a balcony and he serenades her, twirling a daffodil. The girl's father has offered Count Chloride de Lime a million dollars and his daughter's hand in marriage. She throws Charlie a note which says she hates the Count and wants to be rescued. Charlie, feeling like a million dollars, enters her home and announces that he is the Count. The starving imposter is invited to dinner but the real Count arrives in a jitney auto and Charlie is kicked out. Later, the Count, the millionaire, and the latter's daughter drive into the country. Charlie is also wandering in this arcadian scene. He discovers the Count making an impassioned plea for Edna's hand and heart. Charlie throws a well-aimed brick and the Count goes down for the count. Charlie and Edna run to the jitney auto, put a nickel in, and start forward with a jolt. They are soon pursued by the Count, the father, and a policeman. Charlie manages a well-calculated collision at the river's edge and the pursuing car disappears into the water. Charlie borrows a nickel from Edna to start the car again, and the happy lovers drive to the nearest parson.

What was said about
A JITNEY ELOPEMENT

Moving Picture World

There is a vein of romance throughout the story which, combined with Chaplin's inimitable comedy, gives the picture general appeal.

The pleasure of being a count.
(Fred Goodwins, Paddy McGuire,
Chaplin, and Lloyd Bacon.)

Bioscope

Charles Chaplin, endeavouring to rescue an heiress from her father and a foreign count, has ample opportunity for the display of his very remarkable talents. He fights with the agility of a boxing kangaroo, and with almost as much disregard for the rules of warfare, and his motor car is almost equally gymnastic, rendering Mr. Chaplin great assistance in a riotously funny farce.

Cinema

Perhaps no more effective tonic has been prescribed than the Essanay release, *Charlie's Elopement*. It is not only productive of numerous funniosities, but it demonstrates the extraordinary ability of Mr. Chaplin to manufacture about 40 minutes of lively, knockabout comedy on a plot which is practically threadbare. He is admittedly a wonderful bag of tricks.

The imposter confronts the real count. (Chaplin, Edna Purviance, and Leo White.)

The Tramp

An Essanay Comedy Released in Two Reels (April 11, 1915)

CAST

Charles Chaplin, Billy Armstrong, Lloyd Bacon, Fred Goodwins, Bud Jamison, Paddy McGuire, Edna Purviance, Leo White.

CREDITS

Written and directed by Charles Chaplin. Camera work by R. H. Totheroh.

SYNOPSIS

Charlie, the Tramp, has been given a handout which is tied up in his handkerchief. He sits down

The Little Tramp comes up the road.

Bedtime comes early, down on the farm. (Chaplin, Paddy McGuire, and Fred Goodwins.)

by the roadside to eat, but he is so fastidious that he must first polish his fingernails. A hobo creeps up behind him, steals his lunch, and ties a brick in the handkerchief. Charlie is forced to dine on grass, using a tomato can for a finger bowl. Meanwhile the hobo and his companions have discovered the farmer's pretty daughter (Edna Purviance) counting her money. They pursue her, but Charlie comes to the rescue. He swings the brick tied in the handkerchief to such effect that they run for safety and jump into a nearby stream. Edna takes Charlie home with her, where her father gives him a job. After sorry attempts to water the trees, gather eggs, and carry sacks of flour from the grain loft, Charlie goes upstairs to bed. He hears a noise outside and discovers the hoboes he met earlier are robbing the

Charlie considers the pros and cons of joining in the robbery.

The Tramp suffers — not the usual pangs of hunger, but those of unaccustomed honesty.

The wounded hero of the robbery makes a happy recovery. (With Edna Purviance.)

farmhouse. He sounds the alarm and the thieves run away. Charlie runs, too, and is shot in the leg by the farmer. He is a hero now, and Edna has become his devoted nurse. He dreams of marrying her and settling down on the farm. When he has recovered, however, he looks out the window, sees Edna in the arms of a young man, and realizes she already has a sweetheart. He puts on his hat, picks up his cane, glances sadly around the kitchen, and tips his hat to it. After saying good-bye to Edna, he turns away and walks down the lonesome road.

In this film we first come upon the pathos of the Chaplin character, first see his gentleness with women, and first see him in the closing scene, rejected but ever hopeful, walking down the road, with his back to the camera and to us, toward another tomorrow. This was the best picture he had made since he entered the movies.

What was said about
THE TRAMP

Bioscope
Chaplin's art, as all his multitudinous followers know, has no bad patches. An exceptionally hard worker, his natural genius is always seen to the best

advantage. He is never slipshod, never careless. For all his apparent indifference and ease of manner, he is busy the whole time he is on the screen, and his carefully calculated effects never fail to come off. When you go to see a Chaplin comedy you know that you will get your full measure of merriment down to the very last foot. And *Charlie, the Tramp* [the British title] is as good as any of them.

The Little Tramp takes to the road again.

Ice cream cones for two. (With Billy Armstrong.)

By the Sea

An Essanay Comedy Released in One Reel (April 29, 1915)

CAST

Charles Chaplin, Billy Armstrong, Bud Jamison, Edna Purviance, Margie Reiger, Ben Turpin.

The peaceful beach before a storm. (Edna Purviance, Bud Jamison, Chaplin, Margie Reiger, and Billy Armstrong.)

Billy Armstrong, the mercurial drunk of BY THE SEA.

Another meeting of Charlie and Edna.

CREDITS

Written and directed by Charles Chaplin. Camera work by R. H. Totheroh.

SYNOPSIS

Charlie, eating a banana, wanders beside the sea-shore on the Crystal Pier. He nonchalantly throws the banana peel away, then slips on it and falls. He bumps into a drunk and a struggle with their hats leads to a battle. Weary of fighting, they shake hands and have ice-cream cones. In a row over who will pay for them, they smear the cones over each other and over the six-foot dandy who is waiting to be served. While a second battle is in progress, Charlie slips away and begins a flirtation with the dandy's sweetheart. At the end, Charlie seems to be hemmed in by his enemies. He sits in the middle of a bench surrounded by the drunk who wants to fight him, the dandy, and another man who wishes to settle accounts, and, behind the bench, a police-man. But Charlie suddenly throws himself back against the back of the bench and it goes down with all hands aboard—all except Charlie, that is, for he lands on his feet and escapes.

This was Chaplin's first Essanay film to be made in southern California. At his insistence, all the rest of the Essanay films were made there in the rented Majestic Studios, as he had found the facilities at Niles quite inadequate, and the backwoods atmosphere depressing.

What was said about
BY THE SEA

Bioscope

More irresistible absurdities by the inimitable Charles, with the broad Pacific Ocean as a background. Chaplin's humour needs neither description nor recommendation. He is the Dan Leno [famous British stage comedian] of the screen.

Work

The worker hitched to the cart.

An Essanay Comedy Released in Two Reels (June 21, 1915)

CAST

Charles Chaplin, Billy Armstrong, Marta Golden, Charles Insley, Paddy McGuire, Edna Purviance, Leo White.

CREDITS

Written and directed by Charles Chaplin. Camera work by R. H. Totheroh.

SYNOPSIS

Charlie is an assistant to Izzy A. Wake, a painter and paper hanger. The two are on their way to work. The boss rides in a cart, sitting on top of all their paraphernalia, while Charlie is hitched to the cart and serves as the horse. The boss decides on a short cut—up a steep hill. After twice sliding down the hill and into midtown traffic, Charlie makes the grade. At the house they are to paper, Charlie, still horsing around, holds the scaffolding while the

Charlie helps hang the paper. (With Charles Insley.)

boss applies the paste. But the charms of the maid distract Charlie's attention. The boss falls, with his head in the paste bucket. Charlie goes upstairs to paper a bedroom while downstairs the man of the house has his troubles not only with an exploding stove but also with an amorous Frenchman who is making passes at his wife. Revolver shots ring out and the target is discovered to be Charlie, who has been enjoying the company of the maid. He has told her the very sad story of his life as they sit side by side on a bed. But stirred to action, Charlie gives his boss, the Frenchman, and the man of the house each a face full of paste. They all run into the kitchen, where the stove goes into a final, great explosion. The men jump from the windows, the women run out the door. But where's Charlie? Slowly the door of the oven opens, and Charlie, who has hidden there from his pursuers, looks out and then retreats again into the stove.

What was said about
WORK

New York Dramatic Mirror

Chaplin's evolution of what is known as slapstick is the humor one derives from seeing one man kick another and being slammed right back, only the Chaplin way of doing this little service is unexpected and even further is delivered in a somewhat new way. So with his feet, his insouciance, and his every mannerism, which is ridicule directed at himself. There are even those who claim that his ridicule occasionally descends to calling attention to those things called vulgar, but such is not the case here. . . . Undoubtedly the offering was funny, but there seemed to be a diversity of interest, as though it were impossible to finish the reel on the general subject with which it was begun.

Bioscope

The humour is designed to rise in a long crescendo of screams to a climax of roars. Positively, the thing is irresistible.

Variety. Reviewed by Sime Silverman.

The Essanay release of the Charlie Chaplin picture for this week is *Work* in two reels. It is the usual Chaplin work of late, mussy, messy and dirty. Chaplin has found the public will stand for his picture comedy of the worst kind, and he is giving them the worst kind, although as an excellent pantomimist with a reserve of decent comedy, Chaplin must have decided the time to put his other brand upon the screen is when his present style of "humor" shall have ceased to be in demand. The Censor Board is passing matter in the Chaplin films that could not possibly get by in other pictures. Never anything dirtier was placed upon the screen than Chaplin's "Tramp," and while this may have been objected to by the censors, it merely taught Chaplin what to avoid and how far to go. *Work,* however, is not nearly so offensive excepting that it is disgusting at many points, but since the audience will laugh there is no real cause for complaint.

A romantic interruption to the long day's work. (With Edna Purviance.)

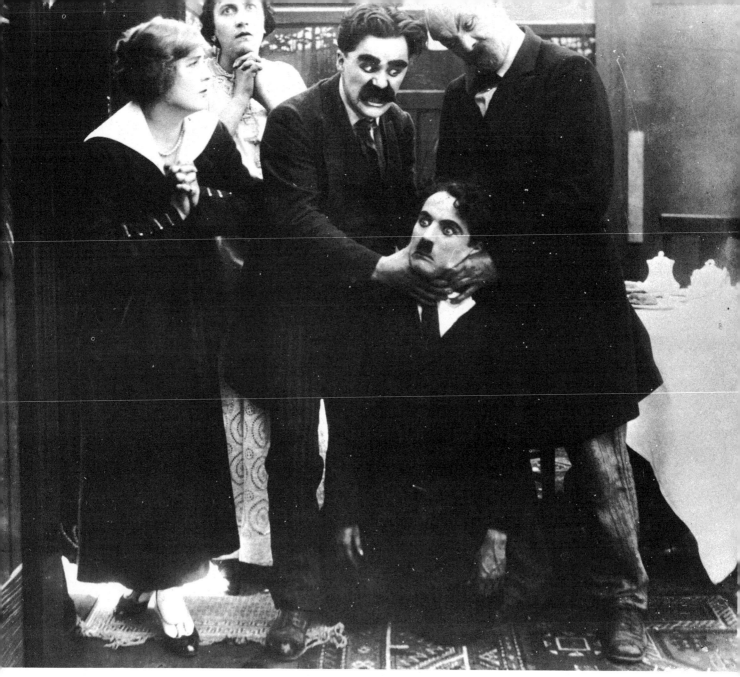

The mischief maker (Charlie) is punished by the thwarted Romeos. (Edna Purviance, Marta Golden, Billy Armstrong, Chaplin, and Charles Insley.)

A Woman

An Essanay Comedy Released in Two Reels (July 12, 1915)

CAST

Charles Chaplin, Billy Armstrong, Marta Golden, Charles Insley, Edna Purviance, Margie Reiger, Leo White.

CREDITS

Written and directed by Charles Chaplin. Camera work by R. H. Totheroh.

SYNOPSIS

Charlie is ready for another lark in the park, but he has made two enemies. One is a man who has

Charlie disguises himself. (With Edna Purviance.)

left his wife and daughter asleep on a park bench to follow a flirtatious young lady. The other is a man who thinks he has already won the same flirtatious girl. The deserted wife and daughter wake up, meet Charlie, and invite him to come home with them. The two men arrive while they are dining and recognize Charlie as the mischief-maker who spoiled their chances with the flirt. Charlie hides in an upstairs bedroom where he finds a woman's suit, hat, and white fox furs. With these he will be able to escape! He puts them on and the beautiful daughter gets a razor so that he can shave off his mustache. Charlie goes downstairs and makes a big hit with the gentlemen. Indeed, they

Charlie charms the men. (Charles Insley, Chaplin, and Billy Armstrong.)

become so hostile to each other in their rivalry for Charlie's favors that the owner of the house forces the other man to leave. He then kneels before Charlie and kisses the hem of his skirt. Charlie moves coyly away, the skirt is pulled off, and Charlie is recognized. The daughter steps forward, begging her father to spare him as she loves him. The father seems to be giving the couple his blessing, but suddenly hauls off and knocks Charlie down. "Get out of here!" he roars, and Charlie makes a dash for the door.

What was said about
A WOMAN

Bioscope

We have always avoided any attempt to dwell at length upon Chaplin films, for the reason that Charlie, in spite of all that has been written of him, is in truth so perfectly indescribable. He is an artist whose genius needs no explanation. His humour is self-evident and his success is infallible. Concerning the present film, therefore, we will only say that it is something of a novelty in Chaplins. As the title suggests, Charles is seen therein altered as a female—and by no means the monstrosity one might imagine, but a very coy and comely young person.

New York Dramatic Mirror

This picture is a refutation of the belief held by many that Charles Chaplin can only do the kind of comedy that he has more or less created, for he opens up a new field of humour for him and one that should be as successful as the peculiar style that has gained him his immense popularity.

Variety. Reviewed by Sime Silverman.

Charlie Chaplin was turned loose again Monday for his semimonthly canter in an Essanay two-reeler. It's called *A Woman* this time, but the title is the least. Chaplin needs a scenario writer, or if he doesn't Essanay does. Too much money could not be paid the man who can fit Charlie Chaplin in his present brand of comedy as he should be fitted. The scenario writer who can do this can prolong the Chaplin fad for months. Without the scenario every time, Mr. Chaplin may as well conclude his finish as a slapstick low comedian before the camera is in sight. . . . In comedy pictures as much fun may be secured through a situation, with the humor starting at the suggestion of that situation, as by the actual comedy work involved in it. That is what is missing in the Essanay Chaplin film, the situation. Chaplin needs a scenario writer, very, very badly.

"Oh, the day that I was happy,
It will not come again."

The Bank

An Essanay Comedy Released in Two Reels (August 16, 1915)

CAST

Charles Chaplin, Billy Armstrong, Lloyd Bacon, Frank Coleman, Fred Goodwins, Charles Insley, Paddy McGuire, Edna Purviance, John Rand, Wesley Ruggles, Carl Stockdale, Carrie Clarke Ward, Leo White.

CREDITS

Written and directed by Charles Chaplin. Camera work by R. H. Totheroh.

SYNOPSIS

Charlie, feeling very important, enters the bank where he works. He goes down to the vault, works its combination with great finesse, hangs his coat inside and brings out his mop-bucket. He is the janitor. He causes havoc first with his wet mop, then with his broom. He discovers a package which has a note attached to it written by the stenographer: "To Charles with love from Edna." He believes she loves him, not knowing that the package is intended for the cashier. He gets a bunch of flowers and places them on her desk. When she discovers they are from the janitor she carelessly tosses them into the wastebasket. Charlie finds them there and is heartbroken. He then has a dream in which he thwarts a robbery, rescues Edna from the vault, and saves the bank. He turns to kiss an adoring Edna—and then he wakes up. It is the mop he is kissing, while Edna stands nearby, kissing the cashier.

Charlie as the janitor of the bank.

Charlie provides a hand-rest for the financier.

The calamities of keeping a floor clean.

Charlie with the girl of his dream (Edna Purviance).

Announced for release on August 9, the week's delay caused considerable consternation and surmise. Had the National Board of Review rejected it as too off-color? Had Chaplin actually made a comedy which was too poor to put on the market? Neither was true, for this was one of the best films he had made up to that time, one in which comedy and pathos were beautifully blended. In this same month Essanay released *Dreamy Dud Sees Charlie Chaplin,* in which Wallace A. Carson drew an animated cartoon of Charlie as Dreamy Dud imagines he sees him on the screen at a nickel show. In the cartoon, Charlie struggles with a donkey, then flirts with a girl. A policeman tries to arrest Charlie, but the donkey kicks the cop and then sends Charlie sailing through the sky. The Essanay Company further exploited its most popular star by having Ruth Stonehouse do an imitation of him in *Angels Unaware.* In this same summer, Pathé, not unmindful of Chaplin's drawing power, made *When Charlie Was A Child,* in which a troupe of small fry actors imitated Chaplin, Ford Sterling, Mabel Normand, and other Keystone comics in a gay and uncorked take-off of a typical Mack Sennett offering.

What was said about
THE BANK

Variety. Reviewed by Sime Silverman.

The Essanay-Chaplin two-reeler, *The Bank,* came out Monday. It's the most legitimate comedy film Chaplin has played in in many a long day, perhaps since he's been in pictures. While there were no boisterous guffaws from upstairs that his slapstick would have pulled, the use of cleaner material brought more enjoyment to the entire house, also left a better impression. Chaplin must have followed some sort of a book in making this film. . . . A few "Chaplins" like this *Bank* thing and the only Charlie may re-establish himself, but he will have to stick to the chalk line.

The rescue of Edna.

Paddy McGuire, who appeared in SHANGHAIED, played in most of Chaplin's Essanay Comedies.

Charlie salutes his officer.

Shanghaied

An Essanay Comedy Released in Two Reels (October 4, 1915)

CAST

Charles Chaplin, Billy Armstrong, Lawrence A. Bowes, Fred Goodwins, Bud Jamison, Paddy Mc-Guire, Edna Purviance, John Rand, Wesley Ruggles, Leo White.

CREDITS

Written and directed by Charles Chaplin. Camera work by R. H. Totheroh.

SYNOPSIS

Charlie, in this melodramatic farce, is hired by a ship's first mate to get three men to fill out his crew. With the aid of a mallet he produces the men. But he too is hit on the head with the mallet and when he comes to finds that he is assistant cook sailing a rough sea. There is dynamite aboard, for the ship's owner and the captain have planned to blow up the vessel to collect the insurance. The owner's daughter, hearing of the plot but not knowing that her father is involved, hides herself on board, having left a note to her father saying she cannot live if he will not let her marry Charlie. Charlie, ever the knight who would rescue beautiful maidens in distress, finds her. The captain and

mate light the fuse to set off the dynamite, and take the only lifeboat to make their escape. But Charlie throws the dynamite overboard and it lands in the lifeboat—and explodes. At the end Charlie and Edna are in the shipowner's motorboat. Charlie says he has nothing more to live for if he cannot have Edna, and jumps from the boat, holding his nose. He then comes up on the other side of the boat and kicks the owner into the water.

What was said about
SHANGHAIED

Photoplay. Reviewed by Julian Johnson.

Shanghaied, Mr. Chaplin's latest ray of sunshine, is just what its name implies. . . . And as usual, Mr. Chaplin is funny with a funnyness which transcends his dirt and his vulgarity.

Variety. Reviewed by Sime Silverman.

The picture is actually funny in the sense it would cause anyone to laugh without offending. That's odd for a "Chaplin," and through it *Shanghaied* is doubly amusing. The picture appears to be following a scenario. . . . Without much, if anything, to its discredit, *Shanghaied* with Chaplin is really entertaining.

The music of the orchestra fails to soothe Charlie's savage breast. (With John Rand, James T. Kelly, Paddy McGuire, Wesley Ruggles, and Leo White.)

A Night in the Show

An Essanay Comedy Released in Two Reels (November 20, 1915)

CAST

Charles Chaplin, Fred Goodwins, Bud Jamison, James T. Kelly, Dee Lampton, Paddy McGuire, Edna Purviance, John Rand, Carrie Clarke Ward, Leo White, May White.

CREDITS

Written and directed by Charles Chaplin. Camera work by R. H. Totheroh.

SYNOPSIS

Charlie, billed as "The Pest," is an elegant, bored, and very drunk gentleman who brings a night of horror to a music hall. He cannot find a seat that pleases him until he takes his place beside Edna. He tries to hold her hand and grasps her husband's hand by mistake. At this moment a gallery god, Mr. Rowdy (also played by Chaplin), pours his beer down on Mr. Pest. Mr. Pest goes to sleep when he is reseated in a box. He wakes up to find that snakes from the snake-charmer's basket have coiled around him. After a duet by Dot and Dash, who sing through a barrage of tomatoes and ice-cream cones, a fire-eater begins his act. But Mr. Rowdy causes the final debacle when he beholds this performance. He turns the fire hose on the stage, on the audience, and especially on Mr. Pest.

The film was based on one of the most popular acts of the Karno Pantomime Company, "Mumming Birds," or, as it was known when Chaplin was playing it with great success on the American stage, "A Night in an English Music Hall." The

The snake charmer (May White) charms Mr. Pest.

film was usually billed as *A Night* at *the Show*.

What was said about
A NIGHT IN THE SHOW

Photoplay. Reviewed by Julian Johnson.

The newest Chaplin, *A Night at the Show,* contains the comedian in a dual role: with plastered hair and respectable evening attire; and, again, in the wildest and most disreputable rig—and an unaccustomed makeup, too—that he has ever assumed. Here Chaplin loses the rails again by reason of no story. And still he is funny. When they showed me this mussy, and at times decidedly unpleasant visual narrative I punctuated it with ribald shouts. I couldn't help roaring. Oh, for a Chaplin author!

A moment of mutual disapproval.

Charlie Chaplin's Burlesque on Carmen

An Essanay Comedy Released in Two Reels, as edited by Chaplin (December 18, 1915), and a Feature in Four Reels, as amplified by Essanay (April 22, 1916)

CAST

Charles Chaplin, Lawrence A. Bowes, Frank J. Coleman, Jack Henderson, Bud Jamison, Edna Purviance, John Rand, Wesley Ruggles, Ben Turpin, Leo White, May White.

CREDITS

Written and directed by Charles Chaplin, with additional footage by the Essanay staff. Camera work by R. H. Totheroh.

SYNOPSIS

Charlie is "Darn Hosiery," a soldier sent by the army to catch a band of smugglers. When he cannot be bribed by the leader of the smugglers, the latter gets a gypsy girl, Carmen (Edna Purviance),

The soldier is tempted by Carmen (Edna Purviance).

Darn Hosiery falls under the spell of Carmen.

to lead him astray. Darn Hosiery is easily led. He falls in love with Carmen, kills his superior officer, and joins the gypsies. But Carmen soon loses interest in him. When she goes to the city with a popular toreador, Darn Hosiery follows her. He finds Carmen, is scorned by her, pulls out a dagger and stabs first Carmen, then himself. At this moment of very real tragedy, the toreador enters. Darn Hosiery and Carmen come to life again and Darn Hosiery explains that the dagger was not a real one.

Prepared by Chaplin as a two-reel burlesque, the film was expanded to four reels after he left Essanay. Drawing upon unused footage made by Chaplin, and shooting a subplot with Ben Turpin and the gypsies, the feature version as released was repetitious and sometimes pointless. Chaplin sued the company, lost the case, and appealed to a higher court. But the decision was upheld. It is interesting that this burlesque of the two films of *Carmen* made in 1915 by Geraldine Farrar and Theda Bara was itself the subject of a burlesque, *Chip's Carmen,* made by a company of juvenile actors.

What was said about
CHARLIE CHAPLIN'S BURLESQUE ON CARMEN (four-reel version)

Photoplay. Reviewed by Julian Johnson.

Carmen, a belated Essanay Chaplin, is a rugged, raggy lyric anent the adventures of "Darn Hosiery," quondam cavalier of Carmen, a Sweet Cap weaver among the nicotine looms of well-known Seville. In two reels this would be a characteristic Chaplin uproar. Four reels is watering the cream.

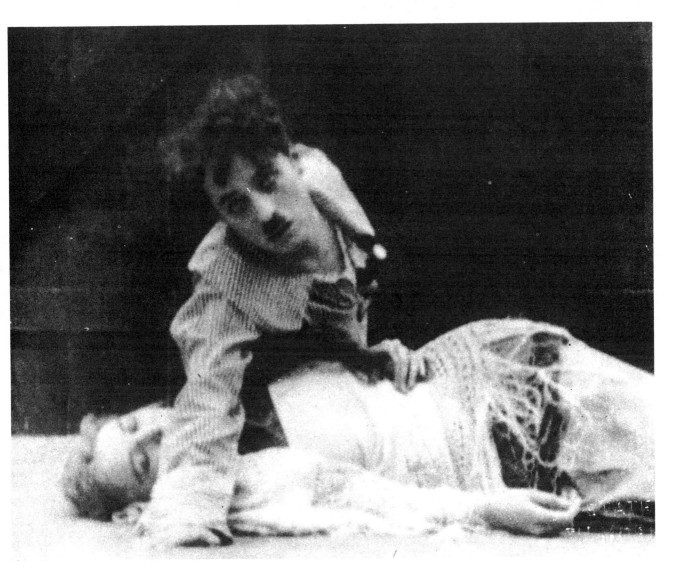

The death of Carmen and Darn Hosiery.

Variety. Reviewed by Jolo.

Charlie Chaplin's burlesque on "Carmen," the much-talked-of Essanay (V-L-S-E) release, was given a private showing for review last week. It is in four reels and, on the whole, was voted unsatisfactory by the majority of exhibitors who attended. The consensus of opinion is that it is a very much padded picture. In two reels it would undoubtedly have proved a "knock-out," for the reason that a burlesque on a tragedy lends itself readily to humorous treatment. There are a number of scenes in which Chaplin doesn't appear, and these may have been taken after the comedian had severed his connection with Essanay. Some of the comedian's own scenes were also elaborated, showing him in repetitions of bits of "business," giving the impression the manufacturer had repeated them in order to pad out the picture to its present length. The appearance of Chaplin in other than his usual make-up also served to detract from the general effect. Clad in exaggerated military uniform and with his prop mustache a trifle short, he wasn't recognized at first and doesn't stand out sufficiently when working opposite the other characters similarly clad.

Leaving prison, Charlie is advised to "go straight."

Police

An Essanay Comedy Released in Two Reels (May 27, 1916)

CAST

Charles Chaplin, Billy Armstrong, Frank J. Coleman, Fred Goodwins, Bud Jamison, James T. Kelly, Edna Purviance, John Rand, Wesley Ruggles, Leo White.

CREDITS

Written and directed by Charles Chaplin, but edited after he had left Essanay. Camera work by R. H. Totheroh.

SYNOPSIS

Charlie is a convict and upon his release from prison is admonished by a fake parson to go straight. The "parson" then pockets the money given to Charlie upon being discharged. Meeting a burglar he had known in prison, Charlie agrees to help on a robbery. When they have difficulty breaking into a house, Charlie calmly walks in the front door. Edna, whose house is being robbed, has summoned the police. But she becomes so charmed by Charlie's manners that by the time the police arrive she tells them that he is her husband. After the police have left, Edna gives Charlie a

Charlie eliminates a cop (John Rand).

Charlie decides he must steal the piano. (With Edna Purviance.)

dollar and he goes happily on his way. He is soon on the run, however, as another policeman has spied him—and the old chase is renewed.

Essanay tampered with this film too after Chaplin had left the company, removing the best sequence and using it much later in *Triple Trouble*.

What was said about
POLICE

Motion Picture News. Reviewed by Oscar Cooper.
Those who believe that Chaplin's abilities are limited to the mallet, the kick and the spinal curvature walk, should see this picture. They will be disillusioned. They will see a touch of heart interest just at the end of the subject, and they will see that Charlie's stock of pantomime includes pathos as well as fooling. But of course, the picture is mainly clever horseplay, beginning with Charlie's exit from prison, and ending with his flight from a policeman. The central incident is the burglarizing of a house, and it is ludicrous in the extreme. Here all the well-known Chaplin tricks are brought into play. After the eccentric burglar and his pal have gathered up everything in sight, the girl (Edna Purviance) asks them not to go upstairs as her mother is very ill and the shock might kill her. The pal demurs, and Charlie is forced to knock him out. This wins the girl's gratitude, so when the police arrive she tells them Charlie is her husband. For a few minutes thereafter Chaplin portrays a penitent, arousing sympathy fully equal in force to the laughter he had aroused before. The supporting cast is uniformly good, with Miss Purviance ranking easily next to the star.

Charlie in the stove, the final scene of WORK and of TRIPLE TROUBLE.

Triple Trouble

An Essanay Comedy Released in Two Reels (August 11, 1918)

CAST

Charles Chaplin, Billy Armstrong, Albert Austin, Bud Jamison, James T. Kelly, Edna Purviance, Wesley Ruggles, Leo White.

CREDITS

Based on material made by Chaplin, most of it theretofore unused, combined with new material made by Essanay in 1918.

SYNOPSIS

Charlie is a janitor who takes care of the house of an inventor, Colonel Nutt. It is wartime and the inventor has a formula for a wireless explosive which the "Pretzelstrasses" are trying to steal. The film ends with a terrific explosion and we see Charlie in that final scene from *Work* where he sticks his head out of a stove, sees his little world in utter chaos, and retreats again into the stove. But the great sequence in the film is in the flophouse where Charlie sleeps. While at Essanay, Chaplin began a feature-length film which was to be a tragicomedy of life among the dispossessed. He was persuaded to stop work on *Life,* as the film was to be called, because it was taking so much time and was upsetting Essanay's promised production schedule. But the flophouse sequence, real, terrible, and wonderfully comic, gives us a glimpse of *Life*. Chaplin had used it in the version of *Police* which he edited,

but Essanay removed it before releasing the film. Some of the *Life* footage, it is apparent, remained in the version of *Police* as finally released.

Although *Triple Trouble* was made up of used and unused material made in 1915 and new footage prepared by Leo White but without Chaplin in 1918, it has remarkable continuity and the parts fit together, almost miraculously. In Chaplin's *My Autobiography* it is acknowledged as a Chaplin film.

What was said about
TRIPLE TROUBLE

Motion Picture News

Charlie Chaplin's tricks in this offering will get the laughs, you needn't worry about that. In fact, I can safely state that they will be as hearty as any that have ever been caused by their introduction in his contributions in the past. There isn't much of a story, of course. The comedian is supposed to be hired as a janitor to take care of the house of Col. Nutt, an old man working on a formula for a new explosive. A count and his conspirators are trying to steal the formula. . . . Chaplin, who is seen in about half the scenes of the picture, appears in his usual wide trousers and his customary mustache. The picture is free from vulgarity. The "kicks" that used to be so common in the old days are absent except in one or two instances.

William Haines, Marion Davies, Chaplin in SHOW PEOPLE.

CHAPLINIANA

Triple Trouble, with its fancy splicing and fantastic doubling, leads quite logically to a consideration of other films which are closely related to Chaplin: the waifs, strays, and fugitives outside the Chaplin canon. They are the films in which he made a surprise appearance, those which were compiled from his early works, and those in which he played by means of movie magic.

Chaplin made several guest appearances in films. The first and perhaps most important was in G. M. Anderson's *His Regeneration* (1915). While Chaplin was working on *The Champion* in Niles, California, "Broncho Billy" Anderson, the pioneer star of Westerns, made a brief but highly animated appearance in the fight scene. Chaplin returned the

favor by playing with him in a serious drama of a burglar's conversion. "It is true," a critic wrote, "that Chaplin is not permitted to interfere seriously with the plot. He is ejected from the story, more or less forcibly, after the first few scenes. Even in the short time at his disposal, however, he assists the tale to make a very lively commencement, which is as novel in a production of this kind as it is pleasant."

In Douglas Fairbank's *The Nut* (1921), Chaplin was seen for a moment, as himself. He also joined the many stars who were glimpsed in James Cruze's *Hollywood* (1923) and billed as the "Chorus of Hollywood Villagers." He presumably occupied one of the thousands of seats looking down on the arena when the studios were closed and all of Hollywood turned out to watch and to be filmed watching the chariot race in *Ben Hur* (1925). In 1928, he made a cameo appearance as himself in *Show People*, a Marion Davies film. The scene was included in M-G-M's *Big Parade of Comedy* (1964). In 1965, he was among the stars photographed earlier in home movies and shown in *Ken Murray's Hollywood*.

Introducing Charlie Chaplin was an extremely short short made by Wallace Carlson, sold directly to exhibitors, and intended to be used as a prologue whenever a Chaplin film was shown. It was copyrighted by Essanay, March 31, 1915. Besides *The Bond*, made for the Fourth Liberty Loan drive, Chaplin appeared with Harry Lauder in a half-reel film made in America for the British War Loan.

On September 23, 1916, *The Essanay-Chaplin Revue of 1916* was released in five reels. It was an anthology based on three films written and directed by Chaplin, with Edna Purviance, Ben Turpin, and Chaplin as the leading players. Essanay claimed that the films had been "worked over in such a way that they dovetail, forming a unified play." The story begins with Charlie's rescue of a farm girl. He gets a job as a hired man on her father's farm and falls in love. When he finds the girl loves another, he returns to the city (*The Tramp*). He finds work there in a movie studio (*His New Job*). At the end of the day he goes out for some bottled relaxation with Ben Turpin (*A Night Out*).

Chase Me Charlie, released in England in 1918, was also a selection of scenes from Essanay comedies, woven together by Langford Reed into a film of seven reels. The title phrase, "Chase Me, Charley" [*sic*], is applied to Leopold Bloom in James Joyce's *Ulysses* and has been used by Mary Parr in *James Joyce: The Poetry of Conscience* to help support her surprising thesis that Joyce incorporated the Little Tramp and the Chaplin cinema myth into the character and physical appearance of Leopold Bloom.

Other Chaplin compilations include *La Grande Parade de Charlot* (Paris, 1948), with commentary by Georges Sadoul and based on *Making a Living, His New Job, The Tramp, A Woman, Work, The Bank,* and *Shanghaied*. The British *Comedy Cocktail*, in two reels with sound, leaned heavily on *A Night in the Show*, with sequences from *Laughing Gas, His Musical Career,* and *The Champion*. A serial in thirty episodes, *The Perils of Patrick*, was fashioned from the Keystone films and released in 1918. *A Night with Charlie Chaplin* and the *Charlie Chaplin Festival* are representative titles of what were merely package deals, three or four Chaplin shorts being grouped together for purposes of distribution. Robert Youngson in his nostalgic films made from films (*When Comedy Was King, Thirty Years of Fun,* and *Days of Thrills and Laughter*) included scenes from the Chaplin comedies. We remember particularly the clips from *Gentlemen of Nerve, His Trysting Place, The Cure,* and *The Adventurer*.

Besides these relatively authentic anthologies of Chaplin material, there have been counterfeits boldly presented as new Chaplin films. They were usually made by taking bits from his old films and shooting new material around them, or by using old footage from other films with which he had no connection. They are examples of what William K. Everson has called "the art of making movies largely out of nothing." Theodore Huff in his *Charlie Chaplin* recalls the titles of some of these impostures: *The Fall of the Rummy-Nuffs, The Dishonor System, One Law for Both, Charlie in a Harem,* and *Charlie Chaplin in "A Son of the Gods."* Three of them had an unmistakable relationship to *The Fall of the Romanoffs* (Brenon, 1917), Annette Kellerman's *A Daughter of the Gods* (Fox, 1916), in which Charlie seems to join the water sports of the mermaids, and *The Honor System* (Fox), one of the great and too often forgotten films of 1916.

The Keystone comedies were particularly subject to misuse because they were not registered for copyright. The Keystone Company published a warning to exhibitors in November, 1914, saying it would "ferret out and prosecute and punish to the extent of the law, all those duping Keystone films or exhibiting dupes." To establish the protection it had formerly bypassed and now needed because of the films' increased popularity, it copyrighted the last seven films Chaplin made for the company.

When advertised outside a theatre, the Chaplin animated cartoons may have fooled some of the customers. Certainly the imitators, who dressed like Chaplin and copied his mannerisms, gave unsophisticated audiences the impression that they were seeing Charlie himself. There was the Mexican actor Carlos Amador, who adopted the name Char-

Robert Preston and Michael Kearney in a scene from
ALL THE WAY HOME, Paramount Pictures Corporation, 1963.

lie Aplin and was sued by Chaplin. There was
Billy Ritchie, formerly with the Karno Company,
who declared that Chaplin was imitating *him*, although other comedians who had been associated
with Karno did not support his claim. Billy West,
of the King Bee comedies, was so clever in his counterfeit presentations that his old films can still de-
ceive the unwary. In Germany an actor calling himself Charlie Kaplin made at least one film. Ernst
Bosser took over the Chaplin attitudes and gestures,
while his leading lady, Klara Kronburger, did as
much for Edna Purviance. And there were others:
Bobby Dunn, André Sechan, Ray Hughes, to name
a few. Even the chimps, and this may be significant, were taught by film-makers to do a Chaplin
routine.

The confusion in Chaplin films has been com-
pounded by the many changes in titles, made here
and abroad, when they were bought, leased, or
grabbed by a new distributor. Even Keystone, ac-
cording to Mack Sennett, sometimes changed the
old titles when it reissued its films. The earlier
films have been copied or "duped," cut, rearranged,
and supplied with new subtitles, which tried dis-
tressingly to be funny. They have been provided
with "grunts and whistles" and a bit of music on
sound tracks which overaccelerate the action. In
spite of the grave loss in quality, they can still open
the door to delight.

Charlie creates a new fashion as
Albert Austin and Leo White look
on.

The Floorwalker

*A Mutual Comedy Released in Two Reels (May
15, 1916)*

CAST

   *Charles Chaplin, Albert Austin, Lloyd Bacon,
Henry Bergman, Eric Campbell, Frank J. Coleman,
Bud Jamison, James T. Kelly, Charlotte Mineau,
Edna Purviance, Stanley Sanford, Leo White.*

CREDITS

   *Written and directed by Charles Chaplin.
Camera work by R. H. Totheroh and W. C. Foster.*

SYNOPSIS

   Charlie comes into a department store and
annoys the personnel with his antics. At this
moment, the store manager and his floorwalker
accomplice are robbing the store's safe. They put
the money in a traveling bag but the floorwalker
conks the manager and flees with the bag. On his
way out, however, he comes upon Charlie, and an
amusing bit takes place between the two men because they look so much alike. The floorwalker in-
duces Charlie to act as his substitute. But the floorwalker ends up in the hands of the law and Charlie

ends up holding the bag. The manager enters the scene and spots him with the bag. This leads to a merry chase around the store. Both men start running on the store escalator—"down the up staircase"—without getting anywhere. Tired out, they stop and wind up on the next floor. The police get into the chase, which ends when the manager gets his head stuck in the elévator while Charlie helps to keep it there.

This was Chaplin's first comedy for the Mutual company, and was photographed at the Lone Star Studio, which had just been built in Los Angeles for Chaplin. This comedy marked the first appearance with Chaplin of a new villain, Eric Campbell. Lloyd Bacon, who became a successful director, was Charlie's double—the dishonest floorwalker.

What was said about
THE FLOORWALKER

Madison (Wisconsin) State Journal. Reviewed by Maxson F. Judell.

Performing in inimitable style on an escalator, or in common parlance, a moving stairway, injecting new "business," such as he has not given to the public in previous comedies, producing the film carefully with adequate settings and excellent pho-

tography, supported by a well-chosen cast, Charles Chaplin proves conclusively that he is without question of doubt the world's greatest comedian. Chaplin possesses that indefinable something which makes you laugh heartily and without restraint at what in others would be called commonplace actions.

Moving Picture World. Reviewed by Louis Reeves Harrison.

Chaplin is an artist of larger capacity, of greater versatility than is apparent to those who know him best. A great many of the screen stories in which he appears are little more than repetitions, or thinly disguised variations, of what he has already done, compelling him to repeat from lack of new business; whereas he would be more effective in some bright and new comedy in almost any role it offered. He has discovered the secret of what brings the laugh, the portrayal of plain, ordinary stupidity. This is illustrated in *The Floorwalker,* where he is chased down a moving staircase which is going up. Some pure psychology there makes it the funniest incident of the story. He needs bigger opportunity, but his personality is so convincing that *The Floorwalker* will win and keep many an audience laughing after it is well under way.

Charlie and the store manager (Eric Campbell.)

Charlie the fireman.

Charlie has a quiet game of checkers with a fellow fireman (Albert Austin).

The Fireman

A Mutual Comedy Released in Two Reels (June 12, 1916)

CAST

   Charles Chaplin, Albert Austin, Lloyd Bacon, Eric Campbell, Frank J. Coleman, James T. Kelly, Edna Purviance, John Rand, Leo White.

CREDITS

   Written and directed by Charles Chaplin. Camera work by R. H. Totheroh and W. C. Foster.

SYNOPSIS

   Charlie plays a fireman and produces trouble in the firehouse instead of helping to put out fires.

His blunders cause the firehouse captain much apprehension. A fire breaks out while the captain is away and the owner of the burning house unfortunately gets Charlie on the phone. The distraught owner is forced to rush down to the firehouse. When Charlie finally comprehends his message, he runs off to find the captain. The owner manages to rouse the other firemen to action, and although they are as inept as Charlie, they get the fire engine to the burning house where they are joined by Charlie and the captain. Meanwhile, the father of the captain's sweetheart, sets fire to his own house in order to collect the insurance on it. When he realizes that his daughter is trapped upstairs, he seeks out the firemen. Charlie personally drives

Charlie finds a checkerboard more attractive when worn by the captain's sweetheart (Edna Purviance).

the engine to the new fire, but loses it on the way. Having no other choice, Charlie climbs up the building, rescues the girl, and becomes her hero.

What was said about
THE FIREMAN

New York Dramatic Mirror

The Fireman is the second of the Chaplin-Mutual comedies, presenting that well-known hero in a whirl of fun and laughter that compares favorably with the best work he has yet done on the screen. Chaplin as a fire laddie lives up to his old-time reputation as a mirth-maker, and with the assistance of Edna Purviance he introduces some burlesque love-making into the scenes which ranks as the climax of comic absurdity. Chaplin's acrobatic feats in sliding down the pole and driving the fire engine are marvelous in point of agility, and his knockabout clowning with the huge captain of

Charles salutes the captain (Eric Campbell).

Charlie is berated for causing an accident.

the house is worthy of an India-rubber man. There is little plot to the comedy, as is the case with most of these fantasies, but the Chaplin antics are sufficient to keep interest alive in the piece from start to finish. His rescue of Miss Purviance from the burning house is a capital bit of foolery, and with the assistance of a competent cast it is safe to prophesy undoubted success for the latest Chaplin offering to the screen.

Chicago Tribune

There is more of soup spilling and of Keystone kicking than is necessary for successful slapsticking, but there is also a certain novelty of situation and a jolly humor in its expression that moves to much mirth. Charles Chaplin is a true comedian who doesn't need to resort to the conflict of the physical to make fun. He has a sufficiently mobile expression to do that.

Charlie watches the captain struggling up the fire pole.

Charlie as an impoverished violinist.

The Vagabond

A Mutual Comedy Released in Two Reels (July 10, 1916)

CAST

Charles Chaplin, Albert Austin, Lloyd Bacon, Eric Campbell, Frank J. Coleman, James T. Kelly, Charlotte Mineau, Edna Purviance, John Rand, Leo White (in two roles).

CREDITS

Written and directed by Charles Chaplin. Camera work by R. H. Totheroh and W. C. Foster.

SYNOPSIS

Charlie portrays a poverty-stricken violinist. He plays his violin for the patrons of a bar, but they are more interested in the music of a German street band. Forced to leave, he winds up near a gypsy camp and plays his violin for a gypsy girl who is washing clothes. Because of his playing the girl spills her wash and is berated by the gypsy chief. The girl and Charlie escape from the gypsy camp in a wagon. On the road they meet an artist, who paints the girl's portrait. When the artist later submits the portrait for a showing, it becomes famous.

Charlie passes his hat to an unresponsive customer (Leo White).

Charlie serenades the gypsy girl (Edna Purviance).

A rich woman recognizes a shamrock-shaped birthmark on the arm of the girl in the portrait. This mark proves the girl is her daughter, who was kidnapped when still a baby. The woman and the artist locate the girl with Charlie. The girl leaves happily with them while Charlie remains behind voluntarily, believing the girl loves the artist. On the way to her new home, the girl realizes that she loves Charlie. She returns and makes him come with her.

In this film, Chaplin revealed some of the dramatic ability which he later put to good use in his feature films.

What was said about
THE VAGABOND

Moving Picture World. Reviewed by Louis Reeves Harrison.

The latter part of this story shows Chaplin in a new role, and he handles it well in spite of the necessity of being as funny as possible. He would make an interesting lead in almost any story if it were possible for him to divest himself of the little tricks which have made him famous. Those little tricks still go, and they pay, but it would be a novelty to see Chaplin free to do without them in some opportunity of a reverse, or much different, character.

Variety

Right from the start you are shocked by an old burlesque bit. This refers to the picking up of an expectoration in mistake for a coin. There is much to commend in the picture, but if Charlie Chaplin wishes to retain his position as the world's greatest drawing card on the screen, he will have to be told not to resort to such stunts, nor the permitting of the leading female support to indicate in pantomime that her cranium is populated with vermin.

Motion Picture Magazine

Charlie Chaplin as of old, with a leaven of serious acting that is very well done. In the role of an itinerant violinist who does some agile antics in competition with a German street band, and who follows it with a series of love misadventures in a gypsy camp, Chaplin rises to the heights of David Warfield in the stage classic *The Music Master*.

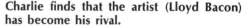

Charlie finds that the artist (Lloyd Bacon) has become his rival.

One A. M.

A Mutual Comedy Released in Two Reels (August 7, 1916)

CAST

Charles Chaplin (in a solo performance), with Albert Austin appearing briefly in the opening scene as a taxi driver.

CREDITS

Written and directed by Charles Chaplin. Camera work by R. H. Totheroh and W. C. Foster.

SYNOPSIS

Charlie plays a *bon vivant* who returns home early in the morning after a night on the town. The home is that of a friend and Charlie has misplaced the key. While climbing through a window he gets his foot caught in a goldfish bowl. Finding his key, he decides the door is the better entrance. Once he enters, he winds up falling on the slippery floor. The place is designed in Early Grotesque, leading Charlie into hectic bouts with the furniture and animal-skin rugs. He finally makes it upstairs,

A taxi driver (Albert Austin) delivers the tipsy Charlie to his doorstep.

Charlie tries to light his cigarette from the chandelier.

Charlie is menaced by what he supposes to be wild beasts.

where he has a battle with a wall-bed which refuses to stay down. After several futile attempts to conquer the bed, Charlie seeks slumber in the bathtub.

Chaplin's film world was one well populated with cops and robbers, irate ladies, inebriated gents, waifs, strays, and pretty girls. This departure into a one-man show was a brilliant experiment which he never attempted again. In the use of props which seem to grow into hostile and almost diabolical antagonists, Chaplin entered a world which Buster Keaton, a few years later, was to make peculiarly his own.

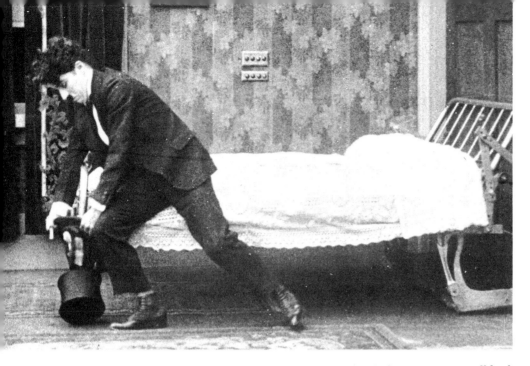

Charlie struggles with the monstrous wall bed.

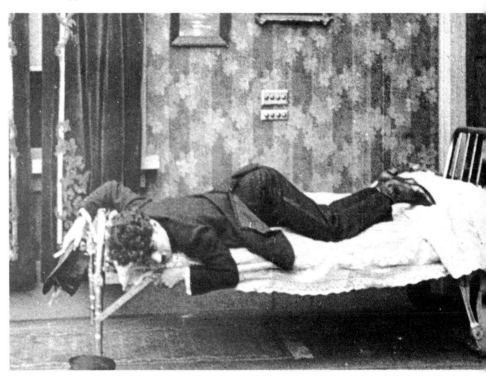

What was said about
  ONE A. M.

Kansas City Times

One doubts if any other player could enact on the screen the part of a very much intoxicated young man for 20 solid minutes, unaided by any other characters, without becoming either tiresome —or vulgar. But the inimitable Charlie succeeds. And he is funny, deliriously funny in spots. To see his struggle for equilibrium with a rug on a highly polished floor is to laugh. And to regard his facial expression when a fall seats him between a stuffed tiger and a ditto huge cat is to laugh more. Mr. Chaplin is so utterly absurd as the intoxicated gentleman that ones loses sight altogether of the fact that he is the worse for looking not wisely but too well upon "the demon rum."

Louisville Herald

Charlie, by himself, creates all the action that is necessary to produce the laughs for which he has become noted, and there is no doubt that this is the most exacting role the comedian has ever essayed.

The tailor (Eric Campbell) and his assistant.

The tailor's assistant tests the reflexes of an impatient customer.

The Count

A Mutual Comedy Released in Two Reels (September 4, 1916)

CAST

Charles Chaplin, Albert Austin, Eric Campbell, Frank J. Coleman, James T. Kelly, Charlotte Mineau, Edna Purviance, John Rand, Stanley Sanford, Eva Thatcher, Leo White.

CREDITS

Written and directed by Charles Chaplin. Camera work by R. H. Totheroh and W. C. Foster.

SYNOPSIS

Charlie plays a tailor-shop worker whose antics displease his boss. The boss discovers a note in the clothes of one of his customers, a count. As it states

Charlie calls on the cook (Eva Thatcher).

The two tailors as uninvited guests at the ball.

that the count will not be able to attend a party at the home of a wealthy girl, Miss Moneybags, the boss sees an opportunity for a taste of high life and decides to impersonate the count. Unknown to the tailor, Charlie goes to the house to visit his lady friend, the cook. When house guards approach the kitchen, the cook tells Charlie that he must leave immediately. He uses a dumbwaiter to take him up and finds himself in the reception room.

There he encounters his boss and in the confusion Charlie is announced as the count while his boss is given an inferior status. The tailor becomes quite angry because of this and grows more angry, as the evening progresses, when Charlie becomes the hit of the party. At dinner, Charlie displays his skill in eating watermelon and later, during the dance, he monopolizes the time of the wealthy hostess. The real count arrives unexpectedly. The tailor is

The "liquid folk music" of the soup course. The tailor (Eric Campbell), Charlie, and Miss Money-bags (Edna Purviance).

caught, but Charlie takes to flight as fast as he can.

What was said about
THE COUNT

Chicago Tribune

It has story, speed, and spontaneity. The fun is not forced—it just bubbles out. A good deal of originality prevails and utter respectability. Some squeamish folks may take exception to Mr. Chaplin holding his nose while eating strong cheese, scratching his head with a fork and washing his ears in watermelon juice at the table. But these vulgarities pass quickly and can be forgotten in the stress of the high comedy of the soup and the dance. Mr. Chaplin has his capacity for serious playing, but he is foremost as a clown and here he clowns superbly.

Photoplay

Our great humanists have invariably immortalized themselves by seizing upon the lowly traits of our native life. We have produced few who can fresco, but many who can whitewash. When Mark Twain, penning his idylls of boyhood, looked about for America's representative in the fluid pigments, did he write of a frescoer—an unsung Whistler, or some Spoon River Corot? He did not. He wrote about a boy, a pail of whitewash, and several other boys, all (for a moment) anxious to be great artists, leaving imperishable splashes on the board fence. So, we have known right along that some day a genius would take our liquid folk music, the eating of soup and watermelon, right up to the Olympus of natural performances. The omnipotent Mr. Chaplin has done this in *The Count*. True, he has spun many a supernal melody from cascading consommé, but these Campbell-can preludes, compared to his reckless emotion with the seedy salmon of vegetables, are as pencil-sketches beside a Meissonier battle painting. When the emerald rind closes ecstatically behind Mr. Chaplin's ears you feel that table accomplishments can offer you no more.

Charlie as the jack-of-all-trades in the pawnshop.

The Pawnshop

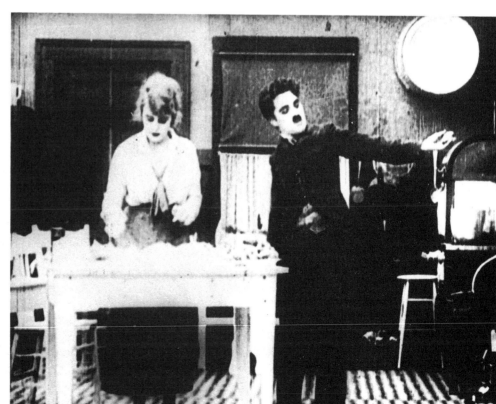

Charlie tries to lift one of the heavy doughnuts made by the pawnbroker's daughter (Edna Purviance).

Charlie listens for signs of life in the alarm clock brought in by Albert Austin.

A Mutual Comedy Released in Two Reels (October 2, 1916)

CAST

Charles Chaplin, Albert Austin, Henry Bergman, Eric Campbell, Frank J. Coleman, James T. Kelly, Edna Purviance, John Rand.

CREDITS

Written and directed by Charles Chaplin. Camera work by R. H. Totheroh and W. C. Foster.

SYNOPSIS

Charlie is employed in a pawnshop. He goes about his job in the usual Chaplin manner, by doing such things as insulting customers and dusting an electric fan while it is running. Charlie and a co-worker get into a quarrel over a ladder they are using to polish the shop sign. The pawnbroker fires Charlie, who appeals for another chance because of his "eleven children," whom he has hastily invented for the occasion. The pawnbroker relents. In the kitchen, Charlie helps the pawnbroker's daughter to dry dishes by passing them through a clothes wringer. When a man presents a clock to be pawned, Charlie takes it apart, then puts all the pieces in the man's hat, and, with sorrow indicates that it is not acceptable. A crook comes in and pretends that he wants to pawn an umbrella. When his attempt to get at the cash register fails, he pretends he wants to buy the pawnshop. Charlie, who has hidden in a trunk after another violent dispute with his co-worker, spots the crook as he tries to open the shop vault. Charlie emerges from the trunk, knocks out the crook, and is embraced by the girl for his deed.

Henry Bergman, the portly actor who was to work closely with Chaplin until his death in 1946, made his first appearance in a Chaplin film as the proprietor of the pawnshop. If Chaplin, in his Mutual films, offered a series of comic essays on the trades and professions, he presented a fantastic gallery of the skilled and unskilled in a few minutes of *The Pawnshop*. A man brings in an alarm clock and Charlie accepts it. Examining it he becomes, successively, a heart specialist, a doctor, a specialist in antiques, a driller, a housewife, a dentist, a plumber, a jeweler, a ribbon clerk, and a cook. It was, and is, one of the greatest scenes Chaplin ever made.

What was said about
THE PAWNSHOP

New York Dramatic Mirror

There is a succession of highly ludicrous scenes with Chaplin the principal figure. One comedy climax after another follows with amazing rapidity, and Chaplin performs some most amusing stunts as the man-of-all-work around the pawnbroking establishment. He mixes up things with a high hand, messes both the outside and inside, and in some amusing celluloid byplay saves his boss from being robbed. There is the usual secondary plot consideration, it may even be classified as third, for that matter, for it is Chaplin who enlivens each scene and by his devious and divers ways of handling each situation causes hearty and continued laughter. To thousands who are yet to see Chaplin, the "Pawnshop" subject will prove an irresistible laugh-getter. Chaplin in working in a pawnshop is enabled to mug, run and slide, abuse patrons, and destroy articles brought into the shop for pawn. An example is where Chaplin takes a clock and piece by piece takes it apart and hammers the mechanical parts as the mood seizes him. Chaplin himself has never been funnier or indulged in more of his typical Chaplinisms, and the cast plays up to him in fine style.

Doctor Charlie tests the clock's internal organs.

Lunch time at the studio—a feast for the boss
(Eric Campbell) but a famine for Charlie.

Behind the Screen

A Mutual Comedy Released in Two Reels (November 13, 1916)

CAST

   Charles Chaplin, Albert Austin, Lloyd Bacon, Henry Bergman, Eric Campbell, Frank J. Coleman, James T. Kelly, Charlotte Mineau, Edna Purviance, John Rand.

CREDITS

   Written and directed by Charles Chaplin. Camera work by R. H. Totheroh and W. C. Foster.

SYNOPSIS

   Charlie is an assistant to the head carpenter at a movie studio. He does all the heavy work, such as carrying a dozen chairs at one time, while his boss takes it easy. Charlie does not even get any recognition for his work, as his boss considers him lazy. Despite the fact that he can swiftly put up and take down a movie set, Charlie does not eat much lunch, although his boss stuffs himself with a selection of pies. Charlie almost gets a pie, however, when he is called upon to act in a movie, but the pies intended for him wind up hitting people on another set. Charlie promises to help a young girl, who has sneaked into the studio, to get into the movies. She, dressed in the clothes of a carpenter, is hired by the boss to work alongside of Charlie, who makes sure that she has help in her work. As Charlie flirts with the girl-in-disguise, his boss is amazed to see Charlie kiss "him." Other carpenters go on strike because of harsh treatment by the boss and set off a dynamite blast in revenge. Charlie is unconcerned by all the havoc; he only wants to keep his new-found ladylove safe. This he does successfully.

   Although Chaplin played in many pie-slinging Keystone comedies and introduced slapstick into many of his later films, he was never hit in the face with a custard pie. He came closest to it in this comedy, but the pies missed their mark.

What was said about
   BEHIND THE SCREEN

Variety

   The latest Charlie Chaplin release is a two-reeler that is to be classed with one of the best laugh pro-

Charlie lets no man upset
his schedule.

ducers that the world's champion high-priced film comic has done for the Mutual. Most of the stunts might be classed with the earlier and most successful type of work pulled by Chaplin. Yet not once does he have possession of the bamboo cane nor does he wear that humpty-dumpty derby. The action, which in no case drags, takes place presumably on the floor of a film studio with a large chance for fun with the numerous props.

Moving Picture World

Set down in the midst of a thoroughly equipped motion picture studio, with the real director tearing his hair and shouting through the megaphone, with dramas and comedies under way, pretty actresses being picked, settings being put up and torn down—there is unlimited opportunity for the wild destruction that follows in Chaplin's wake. . . . While this Chaplin effort will doubtless evoke much laughter from a certain class of audience, it is not one to be strongly recommended. There is throughout a distinct vein of vulgarity which is unnecessary, even in slapstick comedy. A great deal of comedy is intended to be extracted from a pie-slinging episode which occurs during the rehearsal of a couple of scenes in a moving picture studio.

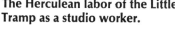

The Herculean labor of the Little
Tramp as a studio worker.

The boss takes a rest while
Charlie does the work.

Charlie the waiter arouses the anger of fellow employees (John Rand and Albert Austin).

The Rink

A Mutual Comedy Released in Two Reels (December 4, 1916)

CAST

Charles Chaplin, Albert Austin, Lloyd Bacon, Henry Bergman, Eric Campbell, Frank J. Coleman, James T. Kelly, Charlotte Mineau, Edna Purviance, John Rand. (Austin and Bergman are both seen in two different roles.)

CREDITS

Written and directed by Charles Chaplin. Camera work by R. H. Totheroh and W. C. Foster.

SYNOPSIS

Charlie is a waiter in a restaurant and makes out the check of Mr. Stout by examining what that hot-tempered gentleman has spilled on his suit. But if Charlie is inept and clumsy as a waiter, he lives another life as Sir Cecil Seltzer, the graceful skater at a nearby rink. He meets a girl there and saves her from the unwelcome attentions of Mr. Stout—who turns out to be hot-blooded as well as hot-tempered. The girl invites Charlie, or Sir Cecil, to her skating party. He makes the grand entrance in top hat and tails, but again locks horns with Mr. Stout. He also falls on top of the formidable Mrs.

Charlie is a good skate.

Stout, but his gallantry does not fail: he modestly pulls down her skirt. The party has now turned into a riot on roller skates. The cops make a raid and Charlie escapes, skating away with his cane hooked to an automobile.

Chaplin's ability as a skater came as a surprise to his fans. But he had once played in a Karno act called "Skating," in which he displayed both grace and a fiendish skill in falling, and in causing all of the other skaters to fall as well.

What was said about
THE RINK

Variety
There is plenty of fun provided by him [Chaplin] on the rollers and he displayed a surprising

The Girl (Edna Purviance), Charlie, Mr. Stout (Eric Campbell), and a fourth skater (Albert Austin) have a collision.

At Edna's party, Charlie falls on top of Mrs. Stout (Henry Bergman).

cleverness on them. A number of funny falls occurred as was looked for, with Charlie outshining and outwitting any of the others on the floor. When he couldn't trip the "big guy" who was attempting to cop his girl, he used his old standby, the bamboo cane. All in all *The Rink* averages up well with the best work he has done for the Mutual.

Moving Picture World. Reviewed by Louis Reeves Harrison.

Chaplin at the rink is amusing enough, but such a vast amount of material is needed to keep a swift farce constantly on the move that this one opens up with the almost outworn business of an awkward waiter who creates almost endless confusion in both restaurant and kitchen. . . . While Chaplin works hard and seems to stand the strain of being funny, an awful strain in its way, he is not given much new opportunity. A man of his resources could fit into hundreds of roles never before shown upon the screen, be even more amusing than he is and provide a greater variety of program.

When the cops move in, Charlie makes his escape from the skating party.

Easy Street

Charlie takes part in a mission service. (Janet Miller Sully, Chaplin, and John Rand.)

A Mutual Comedy Released in Two Reels (January 22, 1917)

CAST

Charles Chaplin, Albert Austin, Henry Bergman, Eric Campbell, Frank J. Coleman, James T. Kelly, Charlotte Mineau, Edna Purviance, John Rand, Janet Miller Sully, Loyal Underwood.

CREDITS

Written and directed by Charles Chaplin. Camera work by R. H. Totheroh and W. C. Foster.

SYNOPSIS

Charlie portrays a bum who enters a mission and is reformed by a minister and a girl mission worker. He becomes a policeman. Roughnecks on Easy

Charlie is converted by the minister (Albert Austin) and the mission worker (Edna Purviance).

The terrible tough of Easy Street (Eric Campbell) sizes up the new policeman.

Street have managed to keep the street cleared of policemen by beating them up. But they have not yet encountered the new cop on the beat. On his first day of duty on the street, Charlie meets the head tough. He strikes him on the head with his club but the tough just stands there, unaffected by the blows. The tough outsmarts himself when he tries to impress Charlie with his strength. He bends down a lamppost, and Charlie, seeing his opportunity, jumps on the tough's back, shoves the man's head into the lamp, and turns on the gas. The unconscious tough is hauled off to jail, and Charlie becomes the hero of the block. The tough breaks jail, however, and comes after the heroic policeman. Easy Street takes on the aura of a battlefield once more. But Charlie is up to the occasion. He

Charlie defeats his adversary for the first time by using gas.

Charlie scores a second victory over the tough with the help of a stove.

was actually Charlie's undoing. It fell on him during the filming of *Easy Street,* and he was then sent to a hospital.

What was said about
EASY STREET

Variety

The resultant chaos and the several new stunts will be bound to bring the laughter and the star's display of agility and acrobatics approaches some of the Doug Fairbanks pranks. Chaplin has always been throwing things in his films, but when he "eases" a cook stove out of the window onto the head of his adversary, on the street below, that

defeats the tough by dropping a stove on him from an upper-floor window of a house. He also rescues the girl mission worker from the villains. Now Easy Street is all peace and harmony, and even the head tough has become a model citizen.

Chaplin exchanged his cane for a policeman's billy club in this film. He made an interesting point in the film when he, a short and thin man, outwitted a big bruiser. Nowhere is Chaplin's respect for the ability of the "little man" more evident than in his portrayal here. The lamppost, by means of which Charlie first caught the villain,

pleasant little bouquet adds a new act to his repertory. *Easy Street* certainly has some rough work in it—maybe a bit rougher than the others—but it is the kind of stuff that Chaplin fans love. In fact, few who see *Easy Street* will fail to be furnished with hearty laughter.

Photoplay. Reviewed by Julian Johnson.

Mr. Chaplin again. He has not only the floor, but a street, and four floors on each side of the street. . . . These diversions make for a merry evening, although the opening scene, burlesquing a rescue mission, is not in high taste.

Charlie arrives at a retreat to take the cure.

The Cure

A Mutual Comedy Released in Two Reels (April 16, 1917)

CAST

Charles Chaplin, Albert Austin, Henry Bergman, Eric Campbell, Frank J. Coleman, James T. Kelly, Edna Purviance, John Rand, Janet Miller Sully, Loyal Underwood.

CREDITS

Written and directed by Charles Chaplin.
Camera work by R. H. Totheroh and W. C. Foster.

SYNOPSIS

Charlie decides that he should partake of the "water cure" at a retreat of this type. There he encounters a pretty girl and a man who has the gout. Unfortunately for the man, his foot is never safe when Charlie is around, especially when the man tries to become attentive to the pretty girl. Charlie also encounters a somewhat sadistic masseur whom he is forced to fight off in order to avoid his rough

Charlies introduces himself to a lovely visitor, leaving a path of pain and outrage in his wake. (Edna Purviance, Chaplin, Frank J. Coleman, and Eric Campbell.)

Charlies watches the treatment by the masseur (Henry Bergman) with mounting anxiety.

Charlie prepares for his plunge.

Charlie brings his own stock of healing waters.

Charlie has a hangover from taking the cure.

treatment. Despite his good intentions, Charlie has not come unequipped for his stay at the resort; he has brought a cache of bottled liquor. An ancient bellboy finds the bottles and partakes of the forbidden liquid. The manager catches him, and makes him empty the bottles. The liquor falls into the "curative waters" under the window, and the guests go wild after sampling the powerful medicine. Charlie also drinks the water and winds up falling into it. Afterwards, Charlie vows to keep away forever from the "demon rum."

What was said about
THE CURE

Louisville Herald

It's a "cinch" that as long as pictures like *The Cure* are offered to make folks forget their troubles, Chaplin will always be worth the money he gets.

Variety

The Cure is a whole meal of laughs, not merely giggles, and ought to again emphasize the fact that Charlie is in a class by himself.

Moving Picture World

To lovers of Chaplin comedy *The Cure* will appeal, not as the best Chaplin effort, but as contrasting favorably with previous efforts. It cannot, for instance, compete with *Easy Street*, but contains in the second reel some excruciatingly funny moments, particularly in the scenes at the baths.

The end of a quiet little game on shipboard.

The Immigrant

A Mutual Comedy Released in Two Reels (June 17, 1917)

CAST

Charles Chaplin, Albert Austin, Henry Bergman (in two roles), Eric Campbell, Frank J. Coleman, James T. Kelly, Edna Purviance, John Rand, Stanley Sanford, Loyal Underwood.

CREDITS

Written and directed by Charles Chaplin. Camera work by R. H. Totheroh and W. C. Foster.

SYNOPSIS

Charlie is an immigrant on a ship headed for America. Poor Charlie and the other passengers have quite a time in the messroom trying to eat because of the swaying of the ship. Charlie gets a chance to play Santa Claus when he gives money that he won gambling to a girl and her mother who have been robbed. He and the Statue of Liberty eventually meet. Once he is in the new land, however, Charlie wonders how he is going to eat without any money. He finds a coin which promptly returns to the ground through a hole in his pocket. Charlie goes into a restaurant and orders a meal, still believing he has the coin. He discovers the girl from the ship there and joins her. He realizes at once that her mother has died when he sees her black-bordered handkerchief.

Charlie with the girl (Edna Purviance) and her mother see the Statue of Liberty.

In one of the longest scenes of brilliantly sustained comedy in all of Chaplin's films, the waiter finally presents the check, which Charlie cannot pay. (Eric Campbell, Chaplin, Edna Purviance, and Henry Bergman.)

The waiter is angry because he has not been tipped.

When a customer is beaten for not having enough money to pay his check, Charlie discovers he has lost the coin. To make matters worse, the man who has found the coin enters, and a tough-looking waiter proves it is counterfeit. Charlie begins to fear for his life. But an artist spots Charlie and the girl and asks them to pose for him. His offer to pay their check is rejected so often that the artist finally lets Charlie keep it. Charlie saves his hide by taking the tip which the artist leaves for the waiter and paying his check with it. Charlie and the girl get a salary advance from the artist and use it to get a marriage license.

What was said about
THE IMMIGRANT

Chicago News
    Mr. Chaplin sallied forth yesterday with an-

other mirthful specialty and thereby gave further proof of his popularity and the reason therefor. Wherever *The Immigrant* invited inspection thousands flocked to see it, to laugh at and with the famous clown, and learn what new thing he had to offer, and they were amply repaid for their time.

Photoplay. Reviewed by Julian Johnson.
    Did you see *The Immigrant?* I not only saw *The Immigrant,* but I saw some light, disparaging reviews of it—one or two by metropolitan critics. Henceforth, these persons can never make me believe anything they write, for the subject of their malministrations is a transparent intermezzo well repaying the closest analysis. In its roughness and apparent simplicity it is as much a jewel as a story by O. Henry, and no full-time farce seen on our stages in years has been more adroitly, more perfectly worked out.

Charlie as the convict on the run.

The Adventurer

A Mutual Comedy Released in Two Reels (October 23, 1917)

CAST

    Charles Chaplin, Albert Austin, Monta Bell, Henry Bergman, Eric Campbell, Frank J. Coleman, Toraichi Kono, Edna Purviance, Janet Miller Sully, Loyal Underwood.

CREDITS

    Written and directed by Charles Chaplin. Camera work by R. H. Totheroh and W. C. Foster.

SYNOPSIS

    Charlie plays a convict who escapes from the penitentiary and its guards. During his flight, he observes a man preparing to go swimming. Needing a change from his prison garb, Charlie steals the man's bathing suit, puts it on, and goes into the water. He then sees a girl and her mother in danger of drowning and rescues them. They are well-to-do and honor the convict as a guest in their home, where he indulges in a kicking fest with the girl's jealous suitor. In a borrowed tuxedo Charlie attends a party given by the girl's parents. Charlie and the girl decide to have a dish of ice cream at a table on the balcony above the dancers. Charlie succeeds in dropping the ice cream down his trousers. He shakes it out and it falls on the back of the girl's mother. Charlie's photo, however, turns up in a newspaper and his pleasant life suddenly ends. The guards from the penitentiary learn where he is, and off Charlie goes again.

    This was the last of the twelve comedies Chaplin made for Mutual. It also marked Eric Campbell's

Charlie, in a stolen bathing suit, hears cries for help.

Served cocktails by the butler (Albert Austin), Charlie enjoys "la dolce vita."

The bed and the borrowed striped pajamas make Charlie think he is still in prison.

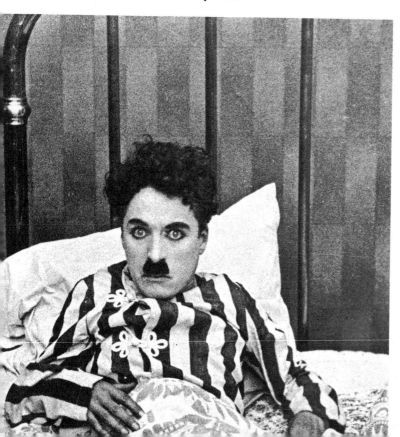

last appearance with Chaplin. This very gentle man, who was the towering menace in the Mutual films, was killed in an auto accident shortly after the film was completed. Toraichi Kono, who played a bit in *The Adventurer*, was Chaplin's chauffeur for many years.

What was said about
THE ADVENTURER
Chicago News

The Adventurer, Chaplin's current specialty consists mainly of footwork. His agility has been demonstrated frequently, but never has he been taxed to such an extent as in this film. He begins by fleeing from jail pursued by a horde of guards, it seems, for they emerge from the most unexpected places at frequent intervals, and he winds up his adventure with a continuance of his flight. In the interim he has demonstrated his dexterity with his feet, his elusiveness and furthermore that he is as agile in the water as on land. He out-kicks his proficient adversary in an encounter and as usual performs mirth-provoking acrobatic stunts.

The young hostess (Edna Purviance) plays for her hero.

Motion Picture Magazine

Mr. Chaplin, in presenting *The Adventurer* as his Mutual swan song, maintains the quality of past risible stunts, though shading in a trifle more on the deft stuff to the diminishment of the broad . . . . There are many clever stunts in *The Adventurer,* and a few very new ones, furnishing material for much smiling, if not for side-shaking laughter.

Mr. Chaplin's Mutual career has been a satisfying one. He has given the company a row of excellent comedies of his own peculiar vintage, which must needs be valuable for several years. Considering that he did as well by Essanay, it is a safe gamble that his next affiliation will be similarly productive of excellence. He is an artist as well as a player of motley. Also he is a—good businessman.

Charlie takes revenge on the man who called the police. (With Eric Campbell.)

Charlie and Scraps. A contrast in moods.

A Dog's Life

A First National Release in Three Reels (April 14, 1918)

CAST

Charles Chaplin, Albert Austin, Henry Bergman, Sydney Chaplin, Bud Jamison, Park Jones, James T. Kelly, Edna Purviance, Chuck Riesner, Janet Miller Sully, Loyal Underwood, Billy White, Tom Wilson.

CREDITS

Written and directed by Charles Chaplin. Camera work by R. H. Totheroh.

SYNOPSIS

Poor Charlie is out of a job and his prospects are dim. He tries to filch some food from a lunch cart and is almost caught by a policeman. He has to do some fancy rolling back and forth underneath a fence to avoid the clutches of the law. Later on, Charlie saves a roving dog named Scraps from some other dogs, and the two become friends as well as partners in purloining food. When Charlie goes into a cabaret where Scraps would not be allowed, he hides the dog in his baggy trousers. Scraps' tail emerges from a hole in the back of Charlie's trousers and this makes the man a sight to see. Charlie meets a girl who works in the cabaret and tries to cheer her up when he discovers that she is disillusioned with life. When Charlie's lack of money causes him to be thrown out of the cabaret, he returns to his open-air sleeping spot, unaware that crooks have buried a wallet there. Scraps digs it up, covering Charlie's face with dirt in the process. Charlie finds money in the wallet and takes it to the cabaret to show the girl that there is enough for them to get married on. The crooks who buried the wallet spot Charlie and take back the stolen booty with some violence. Charlie battles to get it back. This leads to a chase which ends with the arrest of the crooks. Charlie and the girl marry and use the money to buy a farm. There they are seen looking fondly into a cradle which contains— Scraps and her puppies.

Working under a million-dollar contract, this was Chaplin's first film for First National, a company which later merged with Warner Brothers. Most of Chaplin's Mutual Company actors continued in his new films, but some new additions were made to the troupe, including his brother, Sydney.

What was said about
A DOG'S LIFE

Los Angeles Examiner. Reviewed by Florence Lawrence.

Of course Chaplin uses his same funny hat and mustache. These, like the wide trousers and strategic shoes, are part of his personality so far as the public is concerned, and a Chaplin comedy without them would be like *Hamlet* with the mad prince omitted from the cast. But the star no longer depends upon his grotesque attire for his laugh. He shows us in this film some of the marvelous pantomime work for which his stage repute was high before films claimed him. In the scene of the stolen money he performs with his hands, which prove quite as capable at evoking laughs as ever his feet have been.

Chicago News. Reviewed by W. K. Hollander.

While Chaplin was in action loud guffaws of laughter greeted his comic capers. They laughed at his vulgarities—Chaplin does not deport himself entirely above reproach—and applauded his nimbleness. He is admirably assisted by a remarkable canine which imitated its master's morbid and

Edna Purviance with Scraps.

drowsy facial expression so well that one concludes it is a sort of Chaplin of the dog family. This considerably adds to the fun. This dog furnishes the reason for the specialty and inspires an exhilarating dog chase wherein Chaplin with the canine in his arms assumes the undignified role of the pursued with a motley pack of hounds behind him. It is a strenuous chase, particularly for the comedian, for often the dogs meet up with him and bury their teeth into the tail end of his coat, hanging on until part of it gives away. But Charles—not Charlie now —emerges triumphantly with the dog in his arms. Chaplin puts a new dress on some old tricks and renders several comic novelties as well. . . . Above all, Chaplin is without—yes, it's true—his familiar cane. He accomplishes his various stunts unassisted by his adjunct of previous activities. In lieu of the stick he leads his pup about by a rope.

The Bond

Made for the Liberty Loan Committee in a Half Reel. Copyrighted October 4, 1918, by Charles Chaplin, and exhibited during the fall of that year.

CAST

Charles Chaplin, Albert Austin, Sydney Chaplin, Edna Purviance.

CREDITS

Written and directed by Charles Chaplin. Camera work by R. H. Totheroh.

SYNOPSIS

Although this film was filled with patriotic tableaux and scenes encouraging the public to buy bonds to help support the Allied cause in World War I, it also had some humorous sequences, such as Charlie being invited by a friend to join him in a drink, then having to pay for the drinks himself. The incidents were intended to illustrate the bonds of friendship, love, and marriage, all leading up to a plea for "the most important bond of all"— the Liberty Bond.

Photographed rather strikingly against black backdrops, the film was registered for copyright under the title *Charlie Chaplin in a Liberty Loan Appeal.* Chaplin had made a personal tour, part of the time with Mary Pickford and Douglas Fairbanks, Sr., prior to the making of this film, and had spoken at many rallies sponsored by the Liberty Loan Committee. He also appeared, as has been mentioned, in a propaganda short with Harry Lauder, made for the British war effort.

 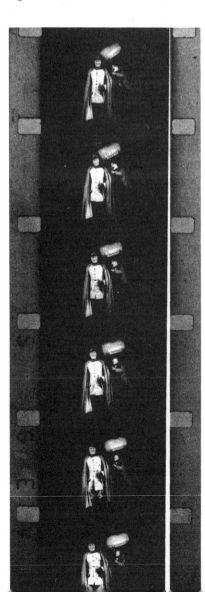 

What the well-dressed doughboy should wear.

Shoulder Arms

A First National Release in Three Reels (October 20, 1918)

(Bergman, Austin, and Sydney Chaplin are each seen in two different roles.)

CAST

Charles Chaplin, Albert Austin, Henry Bergman, Sydney Chaplin, Park Jones, Edna Purviance, Loyal Underwood, Jack Wilson, Tom Wilson.

CREDITS

Written and directed by Charles Chaplin. Camera work by R. H. Totheroh.

The zero hour.

SYNOPSIS

Charlie plays a private in the army at a training camp at the time of the First World War. Although his drilling squad is not very capable, Charlie outshines the other trainees in incompetence. After being on his feet for a long time, he gets into his bunk and goes to sleep. He dreams of what he will do on the battlefield overseas. Arriving at the trenches equipped with an enormous amount of gear, he volunteers to go into enemy-occupied territory. He covers himself with a tree trunk in order to move about freely and has some hazardous but funny encounters with some German soldiers while in his disguise. When he comes upon a shattered house, he finds a French girl still living there. The girl hides Charlie when German soldiers arrive. He gets away, but the girl is taken into custody by the Germans for harboring an American soldier. Charlie, however, stumbles upon the headquarters of the German command where the girl is being held. He knocks out a German officer and puts on his uniform. The Kaiser arrives and accepts Charlie as the legitimate ar-

ticle. Charlie rescues his company sergeant, who has been captured, and sends him with the girl to the Allied lines. Charlie then chauffeurs for the Kaiser and his companions, the Crown Prince and Von Hindenberg. He drives the car to the Allied lines and turns the three leaders over to the Allied command. Charlie is a hero but his dream comes to an end when two soldiers awaken him and tell him that it is time for him to get on with his training.

One of the greatest of the Chaplin films, *Shoulder Arms* was released only a few weeks before the armistice. It was originally planned for five reels and its unused footage has been preserved by Chaplin.

What was said about
SHOULDER ARMS

Chicago Herald
Shoulder Arms is very, very funny. Mr. Chaplin, with his sad seriousness, makes a delicious dough-

Charlie is wounded in the hand by the enemy, but
in the heart by the French girl (Edna Purviance).

The conquering hero.

Impersonating a German officer, Charlie rescues the girl and the captured American sergeant (Sydney Chaplin).

boy and gets into situations amazing even for him. Laughter follows on his every movement and loud applause when he bags the person who is seeking safety in Holland [i.e., the Kaiser]. And when he hates to get up in the morning—oh, me, we feel almost the sympathetic tear. It's a bravely jolly little picture, excellently done, and a concentration of brilliances, in a comedy way, like the light-shooting facets of a diamond.

The New York Times

"The fool's funny," was the chuckling observation of one of those who saw Charlie Chaplin's new film, *Shoulder Arms,* at the Strand yesterday—and, apparently, that's the way everybody felt. There have been learned discussions as to whether Chaplin's comedy is low or high, artistic or crude,

but no one can deny that when he impersonates a screen fool he is funny. Most of those who go to find fault with him remain to laugh. They may still find fault, but they keep on laughing. In *Shoulder Arms* Chaplin is as funny as ever. He is even more enjoyable than one is likely to anticipate because he has abandoned some of the tricks of former comedians and introduces new properties into his horseplay. His limber little stick, for instance, which had begun to lose its comic character through overwork does not appear. Instead Chaplin, camouflaged as a tree trunk, plays destructively with one of the tree's branches. The baggy, black trousers are also gone, giving place to a uniform and such equipment as a soldier never dreamed of.

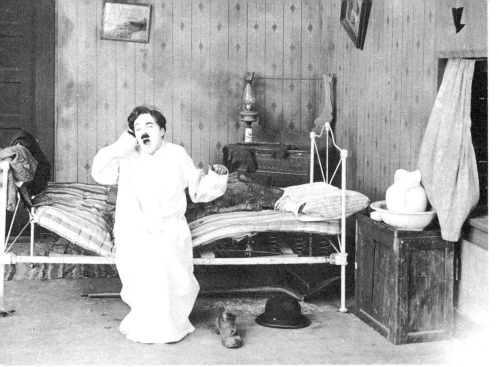

Charlie's work-filled day
begins at 4 A.M.

Sunnyside

*A First National Release in Two Reels (June 15,
1919)*

CAST

*Charles Chaplin, Albert Austin, Henry Berg-
man, Park Jones, Edna Purviance, Loyal Underwood, Tom Wilson.*

CREDITS

*Written and directed by Charles Chaplin.
Camera work by R. H. Totheroh.*

SYNOPSIS

Charlie plays a handyman in the hotel in the
town of Sunnyside. His boss assigns him many different jobs to do, which Charlie often bungles. The
boss is a hard man, however, and it is no wonder
that the overworked Charlie is not always efficient.
While Charlie is bringing cows in from pasture one
day, one of the bovines heads into the church when
the congregation is present. Charlie jumps on the
cow to stop it, but is thrown and knocked unconscious. He dreams about dancing with four nymphs
in the woods. He is brought out of the dream by
his angry boss, who has been addressing the congregation. A man from the city, who is stopping
over in Sunnyside to have his car repaired, causes
Charlie further anguish when he begins seeing a
local girl with whom Charlie is in love. Charlie
decides to dress like the city man to impress the
girl, but only succeeds in making himself look
foolish in everyone's eyes. When the man eventually leaves, Charlie realizes that he has a better
chance with the girl by being himself.

Chaplin's love for the ballet—apparent in his
dance with the nymphs—is more evident in his

A summer morning in the country.

[159]

"Love's Old Sweet Song"
(With Edna Purviance).

sound film *Limelight,* made more than thirty years after *Sunnyside.*

What was said about
SUNNYSIDE

The New York Times

Charlie Chaplin is at the Strand in his latest—*Sunnyside*—so, of course, those who go there will laugh. Charlie is a farm hand and country hotel clerk this time. He is at his best when depending upon his inimitable pantomime and least amusing when indulging in slapstick, in which he is not distinguished from countless other comedians. There is cleverness in *Sunnyside* and good pantomime, but, also, too much slapstick.

New York Dramatic Mirror

There is a palpable effort on Chaplin's part to make serious minutes before the camera conveys comedy, but as Chaplin won his spurs on slapsticks, roughhouse, kick 'em high and kick 'em low and lower pedal antics, the passing up of the old stuff as Charlie always did it lowers his batting average considerably in this latest of Chaplins.

In his dream, Charlie dances with the wood nymphs.

Having used Babe London as a gangplank, Charlie pulls her aboard, aided by Tom Wilson.

A Day's Pleasure

A First National Release in Two Reels (December 7, 1919)

CAST

Charles Chaplin, Albert Austin, Henry Bergman, Jackie Coogan, Raymond Lee, Babe London, Edna Purviance, Loyal Underwood, Tom Wilson.

CREDITS

Written and directed by Charles Chaplin. Camera work by R. H. Totheroh.

The mysteries of a collapsible deck chair.

SYNOPSIS

Charlie, his wife, and their two boys set out for a day's pleasure in their Ford car. Charlie has a bit of a problem during a traffic jam. Then his car gets stuck in some carelessly spilt hot tar, but Charlie gets it free and heads for the boat on which the family is to go on a pleasure excursion. But Charlie finds further complications during the boat trip which spoil his pursuit of pleasant relaxation. First of all, he gets seasick, and then cannot straighten out a deck chair which keeps collapsing every time he attempts to sit on it. Finally, he gets into a fight with a man who wrongly believes that Charlie has been flirting with his wife. The trip ends and Charlie is no doubt quite pleased that his "day of fun" is over.

What was said about
A DAY'S PLEASURE

Chicago Herald

I should judge it somewhere between *Shoulder Arms* and *Sunnyside,* not so funny as the first (perhaps nothing ever will be) and certainly funnier than the latter. You will find it containing fewer assaults upon posterior portions than Chaplin's other films and no missiles in it at all. An excursion on the water, where seasickness, dancing, and fighting enliven matters, is the first reel's task, and an uproarious mix-up of his Ford, traffic cops, and a spilt batch of hot tar on the street crossing, takes up the major portion of reel two. [The writer has his reels mixed.] To me the best trick of all was Chaplin's endeavors to set up a collapsible deck chair. At it he went calmly, resolutely, folding it in and out, until with growing exasperation he gave it up as a bad job and attempted to sit upon it anyway. His tricks are new tricks and his technique the same old Chaplin technique, which is to be classed in film importance with the work of only one other man, the tragedian Griffith.

The New York Times

Charlie Chaplin is screamingly funny in his latest picture, *A Day's Pleasure,* at the Strand, when he tries in vain to solve the mysteries of a collapsible deck chair. He is also funny in many little bits of pantomime and burlesque, in which he is inimitable. But most of the time he depends for comedy upon seasickness, a Ford car, and biff-bang slapstick, with which he is little, if any, funnier than many other screen comedians.

The innocent voyage of Charlie and his family. The success of THE KID has obscured the fact that Jackie Coogan actually made his film debut in A DAY'S PLEASURE.

he Wonderful Kid.

The Kid

Charlie and his "Kid" (Jackie Coogan).

Meal time.

A First National Release in Six Reels (February 6, 1921)

CAST

Charles Chaplin, Jackie Coogan, Carl Miller, Edna Purviance, Chuck Riesner, Tom Wilson, Albert Austin, Nellie Bly Baker, Monta Bell, Henry Bergman, Jack Coogan (Jackie's father), Lita Grey, Raymond Lee.

CREDITS

Written and directed by Charles Chaplin. Camera work by R. H. Totheroh.

SYNOPSIS

A woman leaves a maternity hospital with her baby boy. As she had the child out of wedlock, she feels that she will not be able to take care of him properly. She places the baby in a limousine, attaching a note to the baby's clothes. The note asks the wealthy car owner to care for the baby. Thieves, however, steal the car, unaware of the bundle in the back seat. When they do find the baby, they dump him in an alley.

Charlie comes along and finds the baby. He tries to put the baby into a carriage containing another baby, but fails to do so after many attempts. After beatings by the carriage-baby's mother, he finds the note, reads it, and decides to rear the baby himself. The mother, in a change of heart, returns to the place where the limousine was parked and discovers that it has been stolen.

Five years go by, and The Kid has become Charlie's assistant in work. The Kid's job is to break

The two breadwinners return home.

Charlie and The Kid grieve at the thought of parting.

windows. Charlie then pretends that he has appeared just by chance and glazes the broken glass for a fee. Unknown to them, The Kid's mother is now a famous singer. She has tried to make up for her lost child by helping the poor in the slums. One day she stops a fight that The Kid has gotten into. She urges Charlie to get a doctor for the boy, believing Charlie to be the boy's father. The doctor sees that The Kid needs medical attention. He sends authorities to take The Kid away from Charlie when he finds the note that had been left with The Kid five years before.

The Kid is taken away in a truck, but Charlie, by hopping from roof to roof, catches up with the truck, releases The Kid, and flees with him. The doctor shows the note concerning The Kid to the mother. She recognizes it as the note she wrote years before and puts a reward notice in a newspaper for the return of her child. The owner of a cheap lodging house, in which Charlie and The Kid are hiding out for the night, reads the description in a newspaper. Realizing that it fits Charlie's companion, he steals The Kid while Charlie is sleeping.

When Charlie awakes and finds The Kid gone, he searches everywhere for him, unaware that The Kid had been turned over to the police who, in turn, have given him to his mother. Worn out,

Charlie falls asleep and dreams of what heaven might be like, but is awakened by a policeman who takes him to the home of The Kid's mother. There Charlie is greeted by The Kid and his mother who take him into their home and their hearts.

This was the first feature-length film written and directed by Chaplin. "A picture with a smile and perhaps a tear" was the opening title. It was received by critics and the public with so much praise that it must have prompted Chaplin to consider the merits of making feature films exclusively, although he continued with his shorter comedies until the expiration of his First National contract. *The Kid* has long been considered a classic and would have won many awards had they been as prevalent then as they are now.

It is interesting to note that the Lita Grey seen as one of the children in the dream scene was to become Mrs. Charles Chaplin, November 24, 1924, and the mother of Charles, Jr., and Sydney Chaplin.

In listing the cast, we have departed from the usual alphabetical order of names because the first six players listed in the cast received, *for the first time*, billing in the order given above. The other players are listed alphabetically. This practice will be continued later, beginning with Chaplin's first

Charlie breaks up a fight.

film for United Artists. In the United Artists films the majority of the actors received cast credit on the screen.

What was said about
THE KID

The New York Times

The Kid is not only the longest comedy in which Chaplin has appeared since becoming the best-known figure of the film world, but it is real comedy. That is, it has something of a plot, its people are characters, and the fun of it is balanced with sadness. And Chaplin is more of a comedian than a clown. It is the comedy that has been fore-shadowed by the former shorter Chaplin works. Also, although the screen's unequaled comedian is in no danger of losing his laurels to anyone, haste must be made to mention a new individual in his company, as much of an individual as Chaplin himself, and a source of immense delight. This person is a wonderful youngster by the name of Jack Coogan, surely not more than 6 or 7 years old, and as finished, even if unconscious, an actor as the whole screen aggregation of players is likely to show. He is The Kid and he will be remembered in the same image with Chaplin. They have many scenes together, and every one of them belongs to both of them.

Theatre Magazine

His new picture, *The Kid*, certainly outdoes in humor and the special brand of Chaplin pathos, anything this popular film star has yet produced. There are almost as many tears as laughs in this new First National release—which proves the con-tention that Charlie is almost as good a tragedian as he is a comedian. . . . *The Kid* may be counted a screen masterpiece.

Variety

In this, the longest subject he has ever released, Chaplin is less of the buffoon and more of the actor, but his comedy is all there and there is not a dull moment, once the comedian comes into the picture, which is along about the middle of the first reel. . . . Chaplin, in his more serious phases, is a revelation and his various bits of laugh-making business the essence of originality. No better satire has ever been offered by the comedian than the introduction of his ragamuffin kid seated on a curbstone manicuring his nails; and his instruction of the boy in table etiquette will register as one of the best things he has ever done.

The wealthy Charlie, after a night out, sneaks in unseen by his wife (Edna Purviance) and her two maids (Lita Grey and her mother Lillian McMurray).

The Idle Class

A First National Release in Two Reels (September 25, 1921)

CAST

Charles Chaplin (in a dual role), Henry Bergman, Allan Garcia, Lita Grey, Lillian McMurray, Edna Purviance, John Rand, Rex Storey, Mack ("Ambrose") Swain, Loyal Underwood.

CREDITS

Written and directed by Charles Chaplin. Camera work by R. H. Totheroh.

SYNOPSIS

When the train stops at a wealthy suburb, Charlie the Tramp proudly steps forth from his reserved seat where he has been riding the rails. A beautiful and wealthy lady has also alighted at the station and is disappointed to find that her husband is not there to meet her. She steps into her limousine while Charlie hooks a ride on the bumper. When she arrives at her hotel she finds her husband (this, too, is Charlie, dressed in elegance) is drunk. She leaves him, but later sends a note telling him she will forgive him if he attends a masked ball with her. Charlie the Tramp has a fine afternoon on the golf links and has seen the wealthy lady ride by—which leads him to dream of rescuing her and settling down to married bliss. Having created havoc among the golfers he goes to the park, where he is wrongly accused of stealing a watch. He escapes the police by crashing the masked ball. Edna thinks he is her husband, that he has reformed, and that he has come to the ball dressed as a tramp. She gives him "many tenders of her affection," much to Charlie's bewilderment and then to his joy. But the drunken husband now appears at the ball, locked in knight's armor. He charges the interloper. Charlie, with a can opener, gets the helmet open so the husband can see and be seen. Edna realizes she has been deceived and orders the Tramp to leave. She then sends her father, Ambrose, after him, to offer him help and friendship. Charlie points to the ground and Am-

brose bends over, to see what may be there. Charlie then delivers a swift kick, his comment on the help and friendship of the idle class, and takes to the road again.

Here, in a film which was called *Vanity Fair* while in production, Chaplin plays two parts, as he had done only once before, in *A Night in the Show*. Lita Grey (the future Mrs. Chaplin) and her mother, Mrs. Lillian McMurray, had small parts as Edna Purviance's maids.

What was said about
  THE IDLE CLASS

New York Telegraph. Reviewed by Helen Rockwell.

  Brevity is something else besides the soul of wit. It is sometimes a great relief and a rare treat.

The Tramp enjoys the pleasures of the idle rich.

At the masquerade, the wealthy Charlie's wife mistakes the Tramp for her husband.

Which is the case of Charles Chaplin's latest contribution to the silent drama, *The Idle Class*. The story was written and the picture directed by Charlie himself and instead of going in for a five-reel affair he has returned to his first short love.

The Tramp is unmasked.

But what there is of *The Idle Class* is so good and so funny that one realizes how much better it is to be entertained in two reels than bored in five. Charlie is too clever to prolong an idea unless it is really worth it and his latest picture is just long enough. Charlie assumes two roles since everybody's doing it. He is seen as an absent-minded husband and as a tramp, and it is difficult to say in which guise he is more winning. Perhaps the game of golf in which the tramp indulges is the best bit the film affords, although the masquerade ball holds its choice moments.

The New York Times

Now, refined taste is a good thing. The world needs more of it, and you are not to be scorned because of your sensitiveness. But you are missing something nevertheless. For Chaplin is a great artist, and you may satisfy yourself of this fact if you will go to this latest picture of his, *The Idle Class,* and watch his pantomime. It is not his best picture. It is not as penetratingly human as *The Kid* and *Shoulder Arms* but Chaplin does finished work in it and it is more free from slapstick than some of his earlier productions. The rough-and-tumble stuff has not been eliminated, but it's been largely reduced, and in a number of scenes Chaplin says more by a look or a gesture than other players can express in eight uninterrupted reels. Just watch for that "Oh well, I'm a poor bum and she's a swell lady" expression when the girl on horseback rides away from him. There's philosophy in a flash.

Pay Day

Late to work, Charlie tries to appease his boss (Mack Swain).

A First National Release in Two Reels (April 2, 1922)

CAST

Charles Chaplin, Phyllis Allen, Henry Bergman, Sydney Chaplin, Allan Garcia, Edna Purviance, John Rand, Mack Swain, Loyal Underwood.

CREDITS

Written and directed by Charles Chaplin. Camera work by R. H. Totheroh.

SYNOPSIS

Charlie plays a laborer. When he comes to work late, he gives the foreman a white lily to make up for his tardiness, and then starts his job of shoveling dirt. He does this so slowly that the foreman sends him to work in the bricklaying section instead. There he works too fast; his co-workers cannot keep up with him. Charlie flirts unsuccessfully with the foreman's daughter when she brings her father his lunch. It is pay day and Charlie tells his foreman that he believes he has been underpaid. By the time their argument is over, Charlie has only succeeded in making the foreman believe that he has been overpaid. Charlie tries to hide some of his pay from his wife. She finds it, but he manages to get some money out of her purse, and goes to a saloon, which he later leaves in the company of some friends. They begin singing in an alley. Water

Charlie pops up at lunchtime to the astonishment of the boss's daughter (Edna Purviance).

Even on pay day, some rain must fall.

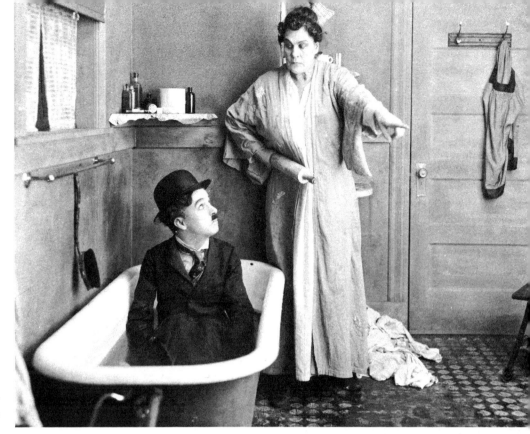

Charlie cannot escape his omni-present wife (Phyllis Allen).

is thrown on the group, but Charlie protects himself from the shower with an umbrella and goes right on singing. Charlie gets on the back of a streetcar to get home, but is pushed up front by others until eventually he is back on the street. He at long last reaches his home and undresses just as the alarm clock goes off. His wife wakes up, and he pretends that he has just awakened and is getting dressed. His wife is not deceived. Charlie jumps into the bathtub to hide, unaware that it is filled with water. His wife, armed with a rolling pin, finds him, and the poor man loses another battle.

What was said about
PAY DAY

The New York Times

A new Chaplin comedy, of course, is an event in the motion picture world, and all that the reviewer has to do is announce it. The rest may as well be silent so far as he is concerned, because nothing can be said about Chaplin that has not been said a dozen times already, and most people are not interested in what is said about him, anyhow. They just go to see him and laugh—and some of them understand.

It may not be entirely futile to report, however, that this new Chaplin comedy is one of his best. It is not to be ranked with *The Kid*, which was a longer and more penetratingly serious venture, and

it has not the significance, perhaps, of *Shoulder Arms*, but it has enough pure fun, and sufficient satire, too, for anyone. With or without reference to anything else, it *is* something else; it is something to relish for its own sake.

Underlying the picture's surface buffoonery is that refreshing treatment of the commonplace by which Chaplin has so often exposed the irony of life. He shows the gods grinning at human earnestness, yet he does not join them in mocking it. He is part of humanity, but has the feelings and the aspirations of ordinary men; he is sympathetically one of the crowd. But he sees the fatuity of it all, too, and so is one above the crowd.

Photoplay

If we ever get to the point where Charles Chaplin fails to make us laugh, we are going right out and order a nice, large, beautifully engraved tombstone. There will be nothing left in life for us. We would blame ourselves, not Charlie.

Pay Day made even the ushers laugh in the theatre where we saw it. Ushers see a picture more times than anybody else, excepting the policemen. It had been running almost all week when we saw the ushers laugh. We can never hope to offer a critique as poignant as this. And Charles Spencer's epitaph could not be more glorious than "He made even ushers chuckle."

Charlie as the Pilgrim.

The Pilgrim

A First National Release in Four Reels (February 25, 1923)

CAST

Charles Chaplin, Edna Purviance, Mack Swain, Kitty Bradbury, Dinky Dean, Loyal Underwood, Mai Wells, Sydney Chaplin, Chuck Riesner, Tom Murray, Monta Bell, Edith Bostwick, Henry Bergman, Florence Latimer, Raymond Lee.

CREDITS

Written and directed by Charles Chaplin. Camera work by R. H. Totheroh. Associate director, Chuck Riesner.

SYNOPSIS

Charlie, an escaped convict, disguises himself in the stolen clothes of a clergyman. He is accepted by the congregation of a small western town and is

Charlie preaches his first sermon.

called upon to preach. His spectacular rendition of the story of David and Goliath moves a small boy to boisterous applause and Charlie, like a true professional, responds by taking several curtain calls. After the service, Charlie is invited to tea and encounters a child more offensive than any of those who were later to strain the short temper of W. C. Fields. A well-timed kick sends the child across the room. Charlie takes a room in the home of Edna and her mother. All goes well until a crook Charlie had known in prison turns up and steals the mother's mortgage money. Charlie recovers it, but his true identity is exposed and he is arrested. When the sheriff and the little "minister" reach the Mexican border, the former points across the divide. "Do you see those flowers?" he asks. "Go pick me some." The sheriff then rides off, but Charlie, with his bunch of flowers, is soon pursuing him. This time, to make his point clear, the sheriff kicks him across the border.

The Pilgrim was Chaplin's last film for First National, his last film of less than feature-length, and the last film in which Edna Purviance appeared as his leading lady. Dinky Dean, the obnoxious boy in the film, was the son of Chuck Riesner, Chaplin's associate director, who was later to direct Sydney Chaplin, Buster Keaton, Marie Dressler, W. C. Fields, the Marx Brothers, Abbott and Costello, and many other leading comedians. Riesner played the crook in *The Pilgrim*.

What was said about
THE PILGRIM

Exceptional Photoplays (National Board of Review of Motion Pictures)

Charlie Chaplin, clergyman, is not the conventional parody of a minister: he is Charlie Chaplin as a clergyman, placed in that position by an accident that does not deprive him of his individuality. He is not absent-minded, and he is not mock-pious. He does not perpetually point his hands to heaven in passionate despair to show the motion picture congregation that he is drunk on theology. He shows the congregation what Charlie Chaplin would be like if he were offered a pulpit and the result is comic perfection without the hackneyed motion picture "business." It is one of the reasons for Chaplin's phenomenal success that he never parodies anything; he is himself, and he has established the worth of his personality in a variety of attitudes and circumstances which make the library of Chaplin motion pictures the unique item of America's finest art, comedy. The subject of *The Pilgrim* offered unlimited opportunity for outworn clerical criticism, but Chaplin was able to let it alone. There are several excellent bits of satire, which retain their sting in spite of their comedy and preserve their comedy with their criticism, but they are good satire because they are Charlie Chaplin's droll thoughts expressed in riotous action. . . . To have written, directed and acted *The Pilgrim* is something to make a man inordinately proud of his own ability. Obviously, the greatest reason for Chaplin's pre-eminence is the fact that he does write, direct and act his own pictures, but that again is subordinate to the high quality of his personal talents. Chaplin's pictures, like all works of sincere art, are the result of one man's effort to use his mind thoroughly in a given situation, with the cooperation of capable assistants, but without the interference of inferior minds.

"And David put his hand in his bag and took thence a stone. . . ."

Chaplin in his brief scene as the porter.

A Woman of Paris

A United Artists Release in Eight Reels (October 1, 1923)

CAST

Edna Purviance, Adolphe Menjou, Carl Miller, Lydia Knott, Charles K. French, Clarence Geldert, Betty Morrissey, Malvina Polo, Karl Gutman, Nellie Bly Baker, Henry Bergman, Harry Northrup, Charles Chaplin (a walk-on as a railroad station porter).

CREDITS

Written, produced, and directed by Charles Chaplin, with Eddie Sutherland as assistant director and Monta Bell responsible for editorial direction. Advisers: Harry d'Abbadie d'Arrast and Jean de Limur. Camera work by R. H. Totheroh and Jack Wilson.

SYNOPSIS

Marie St. Clair (Edna Purviance), a girl in a small French town, intends to run away with her sweetheart, Jean Millet (Carl Miller), when her tyrannical father locks her out of their home. Jean takes Marie to the railroad station. (Chaplin is seen as a porter in this sequence.) After buying train tickets, Jean leaves them with Marie and returns to his home for more money. When his father becomes ill, Jean telephones Marie at the station and asks her to wait in town until his father recovers. Marie, thinking Jean has changed his mind about her, leaves for Paris alone.

Eventually, Marie becomes the mistress of wealthy Pierre Revel (Adolphe Menjou), who keeps her in the lap of luxury. Marie meets Jean and his mother one day, quite by accident. She learns that they now live in Paris, following the death of Jean's father. When Jean finds out that Marie is a kept woman he tells her that he still loves her and wants to marry her anyway. At first Marie is undecided but finally tells Pierre that she is going to accept Jean's proposal. But she hears Jean arguing with his mother about the marriage and feels that he, too, has serious doubts about it. Marie, fearing later recriminations, leaves Jean and returns to Pierre.

When Jean commits suicide after an unsuccessful attempt to get Marie back, his mother sets out to kill Marie, but seeing the girl in grief over him, she relents. The two women become friends. They decide to leave Paris and settle in the country, where they will devote their lives to caring for orphans. Marie is sitting on the back of a cart on the road one day and Pierre passes her in a Rolls-Royce. Neither one notices the other.

In the version prepared for the European market, Herman G. Weinberg says that Marie was quite philosophical about Jean's suicide and returns to Pierre. The working title of the film was

Marie with the man who wants to marry her and the man who does not. (Edna Purviance, Carl Miller, and Adolphe Menjou.)

"Public Opinion" and the change in its title, encouraged by United Artists, came just before its release. In Europe it has always been known by translations of the original title.

This was Chaplin's first film for United Artists, a company formed in 1919 by Chaplin, Douglas Fairbanks, Mary Pickford, and D. W. Griffith. Still under contract to First National, four years passed before he had fulfilled his obligations to that company. One of the main reasons for making *A Woman of Paris* was to help launch Edna Purviance on a career of her own. Chaplin rightly respected her acting ability but he realized she had become too mature to play the young girl of his dreams.

Although the film was highly praised, some reviewers were a little disappointed in Miss Purviance's performance. Perhaps they felt she did not seem French; perhaps they could not see her in anything except comedy. Certainly it did much more for the career of Adolphe Menjou than it did for hers. Before her retirement she made two more films. Chaplin commissioned Joseph von Sternberg to direct her in *The Sea Gull,* also known as *A Woman of the Sea.* The film was shot twice, with Chaplin directing a few scenes in the second version. Chaplin did not permit either version to be released. The few fortunate people who have ever seen the film say that in the leading role Edna Purviance proved that she was a great artist.

Marie grieves over Jean's suicide. (Lydia Knott, Edna Purviance.)

A WOMAN OF PARIS made
Adolphe Menjou a star.

The last picture made by Miss Purviance was a French production, *The Education of a Prince*. It was never released in this country.

Years later, Edna Purviance was to appear as an extra in two of Chaplin's films. He had always kept her under contract and on salary—until her death in 1958. She had played with him, as his leading lady, in thirty-four films. In the two films in which she was probably given her greatest opportunities, *The Kid* and *A Woman of Paris*, Georges Sadoul, in his *Vie de Charlot*, has found a very interesting relationship. He has argued persuasively that Marie St. Clair of *A Woman of Paris* could have been the mother of *The Kid*, that "her adventures are written in the margin of that famous film."

What was said about
A WOMAN OF PARIS

The New York Times
Our old friend Charlie Chaplin, the world's screen clown, has flung aside temporarily his shapeless trousers and his tiny derby, plucked off his eyebrow mustache, and in a well-tailored suit has graduated into Charles Spencer Chaplin, director par excellence. . . . This film lives, and the more directors emulate Mr. Chaplin the better will it be for the producing of pictures.

Variety. Reviewed by Jack Lait.
It is a serious, sincere effort, with a fine story [and] subtlety of idea-expression in many instances new to film dramatization, a thoroughly workmanlike production and a candidate for honors and dollars entirely independent of the drawing power Chaplin built up in other fields. . . . One may safely say that if Chaplin could afford to give his time to the drama on the screen he would run away with it as surely as he did with comedy. In *A Woman of Paris* he hits hard without ever leaving his plot for a second.

The Lone Prospector.

The Gold

A United Artists Release in Nine Reels (August 16, 1925)

CAST

   Charles Chaplin, Mack Swain, Georgia Hale, Tom Murray, Henry Bergman, Malcolm Waite, Betty Morrissey.

CREDITS

   Written, produced, and directed by Charles Chaplin, with Charles ("Chuck") Riesner and H. d'Abbadie d'Arrast as associate and assistant directors. Photography by R. H. Totheroh, with Jack Wilson as cameraman. (A musical score and narration by Chaplin are in the 1942 reissue.)

SYNOPSIS

   Charlie plays a lone prospector who comes to Alaska at the turn of the century to search for gold. A snowstorm drives him into the cabin of outlaw Black Larson (Tom Murray). Big Jim McKay (Mack Swain), a prospector who has found gold on his claim, is also driven by the storm into the

Black Larson (Tom Murray) finds Charlie in his cabin.

Rush

same cabin. When Larson orders both men to leave, Big Jim is forced to fight with Larson for possession of a rifle which Charlie keeps trying to avoid but which continually winds up pointing at him no matter where he runs. Big Jim wins the fight, and Larson accepts the two as guests. The three realize that one of them must go for aid. When a deck of playing cards is used to decide the matter, Larson draws the low card and leaves.

During his trek, Larson comes upon and kills two law officers who have been looking for him. He steals their dogsled, but later is killed in a snow avalanche. Charlie and Big Jim are near starvation in the cabin. Charlie cooks one of his shoes for them to eat, and wraps up his bare foot with so many sackcloths that his new, huge "shoe" seems warmer than his old one. Charlie even imagines the shoelaces to be spaghetti and the nails to be bones. However, Big Jim is not satisfied with this meal, and he begins to picture Charlie as a huge rooster to be cooked. Charlie is forced to use all his agility and guile in order to avoid dismemberment. He gets possession of the rifle and shoots a

The pangs of hunger.

The gourmet dines on his shoe and laces.

Hunger has made Big Jim McKay
(Mack Swain) delirious.

Charlie defends himself
against Big Jim.

[182]

wandering bear, which becomes their sustenance. When the storm subsides, Charlie and Big Jim go their separate ways.

Charlie arrives at a mining town. He goes into a saloon, where he spots a lovely dance-hall girl named Georgia (Georgia Hale) and immediately falls in love with her. She dances with Charlie but her affections are centered on Jack Cameron (Malcolm Waite). When Charlie's trousers begin to fall, he grabs a nearby rope and ties it around his waist, not realizing that a dog is on the other end of it. The poor dog is dragged around during the dance by the unsuspecting Charlie.

Later on, a hungry Charlie deliberately lies down at the door of a cabin on the outskirts of town to arouse the pity of the cabin owner. This man, Hank Curtis (Henry Bergman), takes him in, feeds him, and later leaves the cabin in his hands when he goes on a trip. Georgia and the girls, out for a walk, find Charlie residing there. While Charlie is outside, Georgia comes upon a photo of herself hidden inside. Upon his return, Georgia and the other girls accept Charlie's invitation to have New Year's Eve dinner with him at the cabin. Charlie makes money for the dinner by shoveling snow for one building owner; then, piling the snow in front of the next building, he gets the job of clearing the snow from its entrance. On New Year's Eve, Charlie has everything prepared, but Georgia has forgotten. He goes to town and sees Georgia celebrating the holiday with others in the saloon. Later, Georgia remembers her promise to Charlie. She and the other girls, accompanied by Cameron, go to the cabin, but Charlie has not returned. When Georgia sees all his preparations, she is saddened by the hurt she knows Charlie is feeling.

Meanwhile, Big Jim, who has forgotten where his gold claim is, has been looking for Charlie in the hope that Charlie can help him find it. When they meet, Big Jim promises Charlie half the claim in return for his aid. The two men decide to spend the night at Larson's cabin before they set out. During the night, a new snowstorm has driven the cabin to a cliff. When the two men awake, the cabin, which is already partially over the edge of the cliff, starts tottering as they move to the other side. When Charlie opens the door, he almost falls to his death. Charlie and Big Jim keep sliding on the floor as they try to climb to the safer side. Big Jim finally escapes from the cabin and discovers

Charlie falls in love with the dance hall girl (Georgia Hale).

that he is standing on his gold claim. He throws a rope to Charlie in the cabin and pulls him to safety just as the cabin goes over the cliff.

Charlie and Big Jim, now wealthy, leave on a ship for the American mainland. Charlie agrees to pose in his old outfit for a news photographer. While doing this, he spots Georgia on the deck below. He had looked for her without success in town. When he rushes to her the girl thinks that he has stowed away, and volunteers to help him. When the captain explains that Charlie is a wealthy man, Georgia is astonished. Charlie says that he hopes she will become his wife, and the two look forward to a bright future together.

This film, Chaplin's most ambitious effort up to this time, was highly successful, and deservedly so. In the future, the time between each Chaplin release would grow longer and longer. But he was never forgotten and his new films were awaited with an eagerness rarely shown for the pictures of other personalities. *The Gold Rush*, which many

Charlie has prepared a banquet
for the girls who never come.

consider to be Chaplin's finest achievement, was revived in 1942 with a sound track which introduced a narration written and spoken by Chaplin. A few scenes were cut and a few unused scenes were inserted in this version. It was dedicated to Alexander Woollcott, who had seen in Charlie's "unfailing gallantry—his preposterous innocent gallantry in a world of gross Goliaths—the finest gentleman of our time."

When *The Gold Rush* was reissued with a sound track in 1942, James Fields received an Academy nomination for sound recording, Max Terr for scoring.

What was said about
 THE GOLD RUSH

The New York Times. Reviewed by Mordaunt Hall.

Here is a comedy with streaks of poetry, pathos, tenderness, linked with brusqueness and boisterousness. It is the outstanding gem of all Chaplin's pictures, as it has more thought and originality than even such masterpieces as *The Kid* and *Shoulder Arms*.

New York Herald Tribune. Reviewed by Harriette Underhill.

Praising one of Mr. Chaplin's pictures is like saying that Shakespeare was a good writer. And yet we heard pie-faced persons coming out of the Strand after the performance was over saying, "Do you know, I think Chaplin is a genius!" Well, so do we, but never has it been written so clearly in letters of fire as now.

New York Evening Post

Any audience will be enthusiastic over *The Gold Rush*. Mr. Chaplin has never been funnier, nor has he been more pathetic. The film contains some

The cabin is carried by a storm
to the edge of a precipice.

of the most hilarious as well as some of the saddest moments that we have ever encountered upon the screen. A keen directorial sense of dramatic situation is strikingly evident throughout this picture and there is an intelligence, a sense of refined discrimination in the choice of episodes which wrenches the film at once out of the ordinary level of the moving picture and deposits it securely on a pinnacle far above the average production.

New York Daily News. Reviewed by Mildred Spain.

The Gold Rush collars you, plays quickly upon your emotions and leaves you in that mood where you can't laugh without a sob tearing through or sob without a laugh bubbling up from the depths of the understanding of laughter. It is the funniest and saddest of all comedies. The latest Chaplin picture is like a boy who has grown old without going through the doldrums of middle age. Chaplin hasn't the broad, boisterous note of his earlier work, or the smart, pin-pointed subtlety of *A Woman of Paris.* The new picture is cunningly placed ·between those phases.

New York Daily Mirror. Reviewed by Dorothy Herzog.

The Gold Rush is a box office mint. . . . In spots this comedy sent an audience of blasé movie people into gales of laughter, fairly rocking the theatre. . . . It is rare merriment and another riotous success for Chaplin.

Charlie finds more than gold; he finds the dance hall girl.

The now wealthy Charlie reminds Big Jim of the old days.

Charlie gives his heart to the circus
owner's daughter (Merna Kennedy).

The Circus

Charlie in the lion's cage.

Charlie under the big top.

A United Artists Release in Seven Reels (January 7, 1928)

CAST

Charles Chaplin, Merna Kennedy, Betty Morrissey, Harry Crocker, Allan Garcia, Henry Bergman, Stanley J. Sanford, George Davis, John Rand, Steve Murphy, Doc Stone, Albert Austin, Heinie Conklin.

CREDITS

Written, produced, and directed by Charles Chaplin, with Harry Crocker as assistant. Photography by R. H. Totheroh with Jack Wilson and Mark Marklatt as cameramen.

SYNOPSIS

Charlie, at the midway of a circus "somewhere in the sticks," is wrongly accused of theft. A policeman chases him through the whole area of the circus and its amusement concessions. Charlie's innocence is established and he even gets a job with the circus. He meets the circus equestrienne (Merna Kennedy), who is also the stepdaughter of the circus owner (Allan Garcia). Charlie falls in love with her, although she is not aware that the

The little circus girl tells
Charlie her troubles.

little man feels more than friendship for her.

Charlie is fired by the circus owner when his blunders occur too frequently. However, when the workmen of the circus go on strike, Charlie is re-hired. This time his blunders win him the approval of the viewing public because they occur during the performances of others in the ring. The circus owner does not let Charlie know that he has become a hit but continues to treat him as an ordinary handy man. Charlie wants to be a traditional clown, but at his tryout he is told, "Go ahead and be funny," and he finds he cannot do this. The girl tells the unsuspecting workman that his mishaps have been drawing huge crowds, and that he should be getting a high salary. The circus owner is furious when he finds out what his stepdaughter

has said, but Charlie protects her from the man's abuse.

Charlie now is treated with a great deal of respect by the circus owner, and is given the recognition that he deserves as a top clown. But Rex (Harry Crocker), the King of the High Wire, joins the circus and the girl falls in love with him. When Rex does not appear at one performance, Charlie goes on for him, hoping in this way to convince the equestrienne that he is just as capable as the man she loves. The high wire act becomes a comedy of errors, but Charlie finally makes it safely to the ground.

When the girl is again abused by her stepfather, Charlie defends her and is fired from the circus. The girl joins Charlie on the road. The ex-clown

Charlie walks the tightrope.

realizes that the girl has left the circus because she feels that she cannot look forward to any future with Rex. While the girl is asleep, Charlie returns to the circus and appeals to Rex to marry the equestrienne, explaining the situation. Rex, sincerely in love with the girl, agrees. He marries her and brings her back to the circus with Charlie accompanying them. The circus owner, realizing that any abuse on his part would make Rex quit the show, accepts the couple. The girl demands that Charlie be rehired, and the owner is also forced to accept him.

Charlie, however, no longer wants to be a part of the circus world. Now that the equestrienne is married, he cannot bear being around knowing that she belongs to another. When the circus moves on to a new town, Charlie remains behind, determined to look for happiness elsewhere.

The Circus, although it did not have the pathos of *The Gold Rush*, was accepted gratefully by the critics and the public. This film was like many of Chaplin's old short comedies. Filled with funny situations, it still allowed Chaplin to reveal his Little Tramp character as a warm and thoughtful human being.

In the first year that the Academy of Motion Picture Arts and Sciences made its awards, Chaplin was presented with an "Oscar" as a Special Award "for versatility and genius in writing, acting, directing and producing *The Circus*." He was also nominated as best actor and best comedy director, the latter being a category which was not repeated in ensuing years.

What was said about
THE CIRCUS

New York Daily News. Reviewed by Irene Thirer.

Charles Spencer Chaplin's *Circus* movie is a screaming delight from fade-in to fade-out. It is a howling, hearty, happy, slightly slapstick cinema production wherein the inimitable Charlie gets you more often by a laugh than by a tear. . . . Every reel is a revelation of humor. Throughout, the film is spontaneous, intelligent. Nothing drags; no part is unnecessary.

New York Evening Post. Reviewed by John K. Hutchens.

Charlie Chaplin wrote, directed and produced *The Circus*, and if it is not his very greatest picture, it yet remains that very rare thing in the cinema world; a piece of genuine artistry, for the rather important reason that he is also its star. And the star, as always, is an anonymous little tramp, with a ridiculous cane, a silly hat, a pair of flopping, ill-proportioned feet and the art of that high

The circus moves on but Charlie remains behind.

comedy which is ever and hauntingly on the borderline of tragedy.

New York Daily Mirror. Reviewed by Bland Johaneson.

The Circus at the Strand is a great picture. Chaplin is at his best in a riotous comedy with an undercurrent of pathos. It's certain to live long and be loved. The hardest-boiled crowd in town went to the midnight opening on Friday and laughed off all its mascara.

New York Herald Tribune. Reviewed by Harriette Underhill.

There are certain ones who declare that *Shoulder Arms* was a better picture than *The Circus,* but we find this newest picture at least as funny as anything Chaplin ever has done. The high point

in every way is reached when Charlie is forced to go on in place of the handsome hero, who is a tightrope walker.

The New York Times. Reviewed by Mordaunt Hall.

The Circus is likely to please intensely those who found something slightly wanting in *The Gold Rush,* but at the same time it will prove a little disappointing to those who revelled in the poetry, the pathos and fine humor of his previous adventure. Chaplin's pictures bring to mind the Scotsman who said that all whiskey was good but that some brands were better than others. Chaplin never fails to tickle one's fancy. He lifts the masks from the dejected or the cynical and discovers faces wreathed in merriment.

Charlie buys a flower from the blind girl (Virginia Cherrill).

City Lights

A United Artists Release in Nine Reels—87 Minutes (February 6, 1931)

CAST

Charles Chaplin, Virginia Cherrill, Harry Myers, Hank Mann, Florence Lee, Allan Garcia, Eddie Baker, Henry Bergman, Albert Austin, James Donnelly, Jean Harlow (as an extra), Robert Parrish, John Rand, Stanhope Wheatcroft.

CREDITS

Written, produced, and directed by Charles Chaplin, with Harry Crocker, Henry Bergman, and Albert Austin as assistant directors. Photography by R. H. Totheroh, Gordon Pollock, and Mark Marklatt. Music composed by Charles Chaplin.

SYNOPSIS

Charlie, the Little Tramp, becomes intrigued at the sight of a beautiful blind girl (Virginia Cherrill) who is selling flowers at a sidewalk location. He even gives her his last cent for a flower. That night Charlie saves a millionaire (Harry Myers) bent on suicide from jumping into the river. Each man falls into the water a couple of times but

Charlie saves the life of a millionaire drunk (Harry Myers).

each is always pulled out by the other. The wealthy man is in a state of intoxication and gets Charlie in the same condition when he takes him to a night club.

In the morning, Charlie returns with the millionaire to the latter's home. When they drive up, Charlie sees the flower girl passing. He obtains some money from the millionaire and uses it to buy all the flowers that the blind girl is carrying in a basket. The millionaire also lends Charlie his car, in which Charlie drives the girl home to her slum dwelling. He leaves the girl, allowing her to think that he is a millionaire, and returns to the wealthy man's home. The millionaire, however, is now sober and does not remember ever meeting Charlie.

The millionaire does not stay sober long. When he is drunk again, he spots Charlie and treats him like a long-lost friend. He takes Charlie home with him, but, in the morning, when he is again sober, he forgets that Charlie is his invited guest and has the butler throw him out. When Charlie finds out that the blind girl is sick, he gets a job as a street-cleaner and uses his earnings to pay her medical expenses. When he loses his job, he and a boxer team up to stage a fixed fight at a boxing arena and split the money from the match. Charlie, however, gets into the ring with a different boxer and tries every ruse to avoid the punches of his hard-hitting opponent. He does not succeed and ends up on the canvas.

The cop tells the new friends to move on.

The millionaire takes Charlie to a nightclub.

Charlie has learned that an operation might possibly restore the girl's sight. He is desperate to find funds when he bumps into the millionaire, again drunk. The millionaire learns that Charlie needs money for the girl so he takes him to his home to get it. As he is giving the money to Charlie, thieves knock out the wealthy man. Police arrive as the millionaire awakens. When he does not recognize Charlie, the Little Tramp grabs the money and flees. He gives it to the blind girl and leaves. He is picked up by the police and sent to prison.

When he is released from prison, Charlie can think of nothing but the girl. He happens upon a flower shop and sees the girl inside. She has fully regained her sight after an operation paid for with the money that Charlie gave her. The girl notices the ridiculous little figure staring at her. She goes outside and puts some money in his hand. It is then that she recognizes his hand as the same one which so often put money into hers. Seeing his condition, she knows that the Little Tramp must have had to make terrible sacrifices to help her. "You?" she asks him. Charlie nods, then asks, "You can see now?" She presses his hands and answers, "Yes, I can see now." These are the final subtitles in Chaplin's closing scene, the most moving he ever created.

City Lights has been described as Chaplin's

Charlie enjoys the high life.

Charlie earns money for the girl.

greatest film. It had all the heart, and more, of *The Gold Rush*. Although sound had completely taken over motion pictures, Chaplin felt that *City Lights* should be a silent film. He took a big chance, but the result was a film masterpiece. Chaplin wisely let the musical score that he composed for the film take the place of words. He did use real sound effects however, to heighten the comic sequences.

Jean Harlow was already a star when this film was released, but she appears as an extra in the night-club sequence, having done this bit before *Hell's Angels*.

What was said about
CITY LIGHTS

New York Evening Journal. Reviewed by Rose Pelswick.

With curious crowds standing outside the theatre to stare at holders of eleven-dollar seats who swept inside past a cordon of policeman, *City Lights*, Charlie Chaplin's first picture in two years, opened at the George M. Cohan Theatre last evening and proved that silence—if it's Chaplin who's silent—is still golden.

City Lights has no dialogue. And it's just as well, because if the picture had had words, the laughs and applause of last evening's audience would have drowned them out.

New York Herald Tribune. Reviewed by Richard Watts, Jr.

City Lights is important because it is a very brilliant film, a genuinely hilarious comedy which shows the Great Man of the Cinema in his happiest and most characteristic moods. . . . The unhappy, bedraggled figure that is Chaplin achieves here the synthesis that it has long been striving for. "Charlot" is at last completely and valiantly the combination of the heroic and the hilarious he has been, in the past, able to portray only at moments.

The New York Times. Reviewed by Mordaunt Hall.

It is a film worked out with admirable artistry, and while Chaplin stoops to conquer, as he has invariably done, he achieves success. Although the Little Tramp in this *City Lights* is more respectable than usual, owing to circumstances in the story, he begins and ends with the same old clothes, looking, in fact, a trifle more bedraggled in the last scene than in most others of his comedies.

Charlie in the ring with a tough fighter (Hank Mann) holds off the moment of defeat.

The trials in the life of a street cleaner.

Charlie brings food—and happiness—to the blind girl.

After seeing this film, James Agate, British critic, wrote, "All I know about Mr. Chaplin, and all I ever want to know, is that, measuring my words and remembering all the great players, he is, in my view, the greatest of them all."

New York Evening Post. Reviewed by Thornton Delehanty.

If Chaplin has not attempted to depart from his traditional portrayal, in this picture he has brightened the halos that cling to his earlier achievements. *City Lights* confirms the indestructibility of Chaplin's art, not only as actor but as director. And he has done it without making any concessions to dialogue; he remains the supreme pantomimist. The invention of sound recording has served merely as an aid to comic effects; he can make you shriek with delight by his use of sounds, but words are a superfluity. As long as he continues to make pictures he can afford to ignore the talkies.

New York Daily News. Reviewed by Irene Thirer.

City Lights is excruciatingly funny and terribly, terribly sad. It makes you chuckle hysterically. You have the greatest time imaginable, and yet, occasionally you find little hurty lumps in your throat. . . . We love Mr. Chaplin because he is the clown. We'd love any other artist who might give us this delightful character. And yet we don't believe there's another man in the world who can do it. Charlie is the one and only! He'll always be the one and only.

Chaplin, with Paulette Goddard, in MODERN TIMES.

Modern Times

A United Artists Release—85 Minutes (February 5, 1936)

CAST

Charles Chaplin, Paulette Goddard, Henry Berg- *man, Chester Conklin, Stanley Sanford, Hank Mann, Louis Natheaux, Allan Garcia, Richard Alexander, Heinie Conklin, Lloyd Ingraham, Edward Kimball, Wilfred Lucas, Mira McKinney, John Rand, Walter James, Dr. Cecil Reynolds.*

A worker in the modern world.

CREDITS

Written, produced, and directed by Charles Chaplin, with Carter De Haven and Henry Bergman as assistant directors. Photography by R. H. Totheroh and Ira Morgan. Music composed by Charles Chaplin. Musical direction by Alfred Newman.

SYNOPSIS

Charlie is caught up in the machine age. He is a factory worker whose job is to tighten bolts on a moving belt. Charlie and a co-worker (Chester Conklin) get caught in a huge machine while oiling it, but after passing safely through its wheels, they are set on the ground once again. Charlie is chosen to test a new machine which will feed lunch to a worker in a short period of time. But the various feeding mechanisms on the machine go haywire, all except the mouth-wiper which always seems to work. Charlie is extricated from the machine and put back to work. His routine, mechanical job unbalances his mind and he runs amuck

Charlie's pal (Chester Conklin) becomes a cog in the wheel.

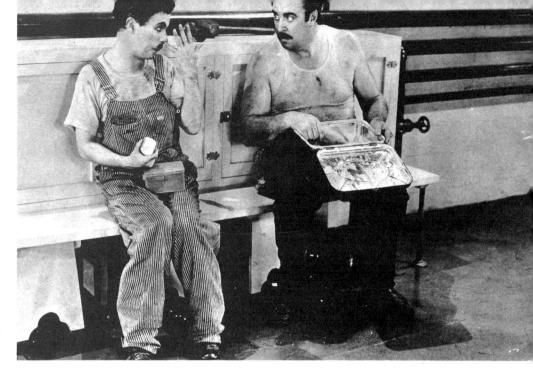

Lunch time in the factory with a co-worker (Stanley Sanford).

with a wrench intending to tighten anything round. When he chases a woman with big round buttons on her dress down the street, he is arrested and placed in a mental hospital.

When he is released, he finally succeeds in getting a job, but he has worked only a few hours when a strike is called. He is mistaken for the leader of a mob demonstrating in the street when he picks up a red flag which has fallen from a truck. He is carted off to jail, where he finds his burly cellmate knitting. He is somewhat discon-

certed by this. When he prevents a jailbreak, however, he is rewarded with a private cell and is treated royally. He is pardoned, but longs for the security of his jail cell when he finds that life on the outside is far from easy.

A young orphan girl (Paulette Goddard), who has fled from her waterfront home to avoid being placed in an orphanage, is arrested for stealing some food. When Charlie sees this, he tells the policeman that he did it, hoping that he will be put back in jail. When he fails to convince the

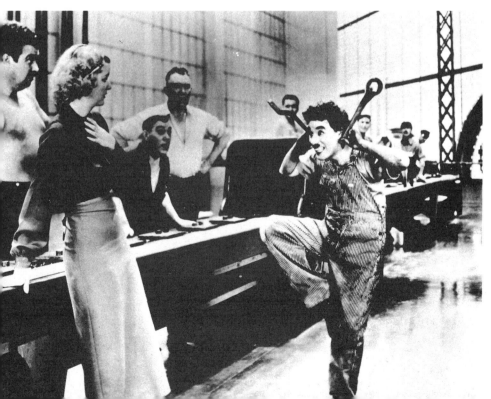

Charlie as a victim of automation goes berserk.

[199]

**Charlie inadvertently becomes the leader of
a demonstration when he picks up a red flag.**

policeman, he goes into a café, orders a huge meal, and then says he cannot pay for it. He is arrested and placed in the same police wagon as the young girl. She breaks out of it and takes Charlie with her, although he goes unwillingly.

Charlie gets a job in a department store as a night watchman. He lets the girl have the run of the store while he is on duty. Thieves enter one night, but when Charlie recognizes them as his former co-workers in the factory, out of work and money, he joins them in a party at the expense of the store. Morning comes, and the jig is up. Charlie winds up back behind the bars.

The girl finds a job as a cabaret dancer while Charlie is in jail. When he is released she sees to it that he finds a job as a waiter in the same place.

Charlie finds comfort in jail.

Charlie is not too successful serving food, but he is a big success as a singing waiter. His happiness, however, is short-lived. Police officers arrive, looking for the orphan, and Charlie and the girl are forced to flee. When they are safe on the road, they talk about having a better life some day, and decide to trust in the future.

The first subtitle of the film reads: *"Modern Times* is a story of industry, of individual enterprise—of humanity crusading in pursuit of happiness."* It was Chaplin's last film without dialogue. It did have sound-effects in certain scenes, and Chaplin's voice was heard when he sang a little ditty to the tune of "Titina" in his singing waiter sequence. As in *City Lights,* his own musical score was used in place of dialogue to bring out the mood of each scene. Dr. Cecil Reynolds, Chaplin's friend and physician, played the bit role of a minister visiting the prison.

At the end of *Modern Times* we see Charlie walking toward the horizon as he had done in many other films. But this time he was not alone. He had the little waif whom he called "the gamin" as his companion, and he held her hand lovingly. "We'll get along," they told each other, and they made us believe they would. No one realized it at the time, but in that moment of hopefulness we were

Charlie's smile fails to win a visitor (Mira McKinney) to the jail.

Charlie befriends the orphan
girl (Paulette Goddard).

seeing Charlie the Little Tramp for the last time. There were to be moments in *The Great Dictator* when the little Jewish barber was to remind us of the Charlie we used to know, then the image faded and disappeared. Only the old films remained, but in them the Little Tramp would always live. He would be skating on the rink, eating the watermelon, examining the alarm clock, dining on his shoe, dancing with the nymphs, rescuing Edna, and walking down the lonesome road as long as film endured.

What was said about
MODERN TIMES

New York Post. Reviewed by Thornton Delehanty.

The gorgeous spoofing, the annihilating inventiveness of the comedy, comes from Chaplin rather than from his material. The picture is a brilliant succession of gags and stunts, strung together on the priceless tradition of Chaplin himself. His story is not so much a satiric thrust at the machine age as it is an employment of machinery as a field for comedy. . . . There is no doubt that *Modern Times* is the season's motion picture event.

The New York Times. Reviewed by Frank S. Nugent.

Sociological concept? Maybe. But a rousing, rib-tickling, gag-bestrewn jest for all that and in the best Chaplin manner. . . . This morning there is good news. Chaplin is back again.

Charlie becomes the night watchman
of a department store.

Charlie and the girl have brief careers in a cabaret.

New York Evening Journal. Reviewed by Rose Pelswick.

It's curious, these days, to see the lips of actors move and to hear no sound, but the lack of talk is almost unnoticed whenever the picture resolves itself into characteristic Chaplin slapstick and mimicry.

And *Modern Times* is, for the most part, fast-moving and frequently hilarious action.

New York Daily News. Reviewed by Kate Cameron.

There is nothing new about *Modern Times* ex-

cept the title. All the old gags are brought out and dusted off for use. But they are such good old standbys that they still earn laughs. Chaplin has stuck to his traditional way of making comedies by working strictly in pantomime himself and by having most of his cast follow suit.

New York Herald Tribune. Reviewed by Richard Watts, Jr.

The cinema's First Immortal returns to us after an absence of almost five years in a comedy for fun-lovers, egalitarians and philosophers.

Charlie and the girl walk on toward a brighter tomorrow.

Chaplin as the Jewish barber.

The Great Dictator

A United Artists Release—126 Minutes (October 15, 1940)

CAST

People of the Palace: *Charles Chaplin, Jack Oakie, Reginald Gardiner, Henry Daniell, Billy Gilbert, Grace Hayle, Carter De Haven.*

People of the Ghetto: *Charles Chaplin, Paulette Goddard, Maurice Moscovich, Emma Dunn, Ber-* nard Gorcey, Paul Weigel.

And: *Chester Conklin, Esther Michelson, Hank Mann, Florence Wright, Eddie Gribbon, Robert O. Davis (Rudolph Anders), Eddie Dunn, Peter Lynn, Nita Pike, Richard Alexander, Lucien Prival, Leo White.*

CREDITS

Written, produced, and directed by Charles

Chaplin as the dictator Hynkel.

Chaplin, with Dan James, Wheeler Dryden, and Bob Meltzer as assistant directors. Photography by R. H. Totheroh and Karl Struss. Music by Chaplin, musical direction by Meredith Willson.

SYNOPSIS

The country of Tomania loses the war in 1918, but this means very little to a Jewish barber (Charles Chaplin), one of the Tomanian soldiers. He suffers from amnesia for the next two decades and is therefore unaware that his exact double, a blusterer named Hynkel (Charles Chaplin), has made himself Dictator of Tomania.

Hynkel and his staff have succeeded in gaining power by promising the people everything but delivering nothing. To keep the minds of the populace off the economic problems in Tomania, Hynkel encourages anti-Semitism. Meanwhile, the barber escapes from the hospital in which he has been confined for many years and returns to his barber shop in a Jewish ghetto. When Hynkel's men come along and paint the word "Jew" on his barber-shop window, the puzzled barber simply wipes it off. A battle begins, with the barber throwing paint on his attackers. An impoverished girl of the ghetto named Hannah (Paulette Goddard) comes to the

Schultz (Reginald Gardiner) and the barber become wartime friends.

barber's aid, but the odds are against the little man. He is, however, rescued by Schultz (Reginald Gardiner), one of Hynkel's men, who served with the barber during the 1918 war.

Things, in general, improve for the Jewish population because Hynkel needs a loan from a Jewish financier in order to invade Austerlich, which borders on Tomania. For a time everything is peaceful in the ghetto because the persecution is ended, but when Hynkel is refused the loan, he renews his attack on the Jewish people. Schultz disagrees with Hynkel and is placed under arrest. He escapes and takes refuge with the barber in the ghetto, but both are caught and placed in a concentration camp. Hannah manages to escape to Austerlich.

Hynkel has his problems when he decides to invade Austerlich. The most pressing is Napaloni (Jack Oakie), Dictator of Bacteria and Hynkel's rival. Hynkel sets up a meeting with Napaloni in order to win him over. He intends to give Napaloni an inferiority complex, but Napaloni is as noisy and blustery as Hynkel. At a party, Hynkel is even forced to dance with the overstuffed Madame Napaloni (Grace Hayle). Finally Hynkel and Napaloni come to terms.

Hynkel goes out in a boat to do some duck-shooting so that the people of Austerlich will not suspect that his men are ready to invade their country. He is not aware that his double, the barber, has escaped with Schultz from the concentration camp nearby. When Hynkel falls from his boat after

shooting at a duck, he swims to shore and is arrested by guards who believe he is the escaped barber. On the other hand, the barber is mistaken for Hynkel and, with Schultz, is taken to make a radio broadcast about the invasion of Austerlich.

The barber makes a speech, but he declares he does not want to take Austerlich or any other country. He pleads for all people to follow the path of peace, brotherhood, and democracy. He mentions Hannah's name and tells her to look forward to a better future. Hannah, whose home has already been ransacked by Hynkel's men, realizes that it is the barber speaking. She silently hopes that he will restore Tomania to normalcy and decency.

Chaplin chose to make his first sound film with dialogue an attack on Fascism and its leading exponent of that day, Hitler. It took a great deal of courage to go into production of this film in the late thirties, when it was still thought that Hitler could be pacified. Events were to prove that Chaplin did not begin soon enough; his message to the world came too late for it to change men's minds. He painted a devastating portrait of Hitler on film, describing him as a loudmouthed, fanatical buffoon. Chaplin did not know that Hitler's racist policies included the mass slaughter of Jews; if he had, *The Great Dictator* probably would never have been made as a comic satire.

Since the time-lag between each of Chaplin's later films was so great, it meant that with each

The rise of the Dictator.

film a new generation of children would be seeing Chaplin for the first time. Parents who had loved the Chaplin films in their own childhood and had grown up thinking of Charlie as a very important part of their world were curious about their children's reactions. They were particularly interested in observing their response to *The Great Dictator*. Many critics had found it difficult to accept the "new" Chaplin and had resented the final scene, in which he spoke not as the little Jewish barber but as Charles Chaplin, making a serious statement of what was in his heart. If the Young Reviewers of the National Board of Review, aged nine to fifteen, were typical, children felt that the picture was excellent. They approached it with understanding,

and liked best of all Chaplin's final message. One nine-year-old boy described it as "his speech to be kind to everyone." Another boy, thirteen years old, said, "I liked the picture because it was down to earth and it shows the suffering of the people in Europe, and it shows Charlie Chaplin's true character."

Chaplin was nominated as best actor and as writer of the best original screenplay at the time of the Academy awards of 1940. For his portrayal of Napaloni, Jack Oakie was nominated as best supporting actor. Meredith Willson received a nomination for the best original score. *The Great Dictator* was nominated as best picture of the year.

Hynkel with his henchman, Herring (Billy Gilbert).

THE GREAT DICTATOR

The New York Times. Reviewed by Bosley Crowther.

No event in the history of the screen has ever been anticipated with more hopeful excitement than the premiere of this film, which occurred simultaneously at the Astor and Capitol Theatres; no picture ever made has promised more momentous consequences. The prospect of little "Charlot," the most universally loved character in all the world, directing his superlative talent for ridicule against the most dangerously evil man alive has loomed as a titanic jest, a transcendent paradox. And the happy report this morning is that it comes off magnificently. *The Great Dictator* may not be the finest picture ever made—in fact, it possesses several disappointing shortcomings. But, despite them, it turns out to be a truly superb accomplishment by a truly great artist—and, from one point of view, perhaps the most significant film ever produced.

The barber protects Hannah (Paulette Goddard) from the Storm troopers (Hank Mann and Eddie Gribbon).

The barber decides to improve Hannah's appearance.

New York World-Telegram. Reviewed by William Boehnel.

The Great Dictator is an expression of Chaplin's beliefs. He hates war, loathes intolerance and cruelty, asks only that man should be allowed to live in peace and friendliness with his fellow-man. But this creed is expressed in a confused manner in *The Great Dictator,* where emotion runs riot at the expense of good picture-making.

But confused or not, you cannot discount Chaplin's sincerity. What he says against dictators he says with the brass-knuckled directness of one whose welled-up scorn and contempt have finally reached the breaking point. Some of this he tells with all the brilliance of the old-time Chaplin. Sequence after sequence—notably those in Hynkel's meeting and dealings with Napaloni—have all the lively imagination and fresh inventiveness which made his old films the slapstick masterpieces they were.

New York Herald Tribune. Reviewed by Howard Barnes.

The incomparable Charles Chaplin is back on the screen in an extraordinary film. *The Great Dictator,* which opened simultaneously last night at the Astor and the Capitol, is a savage comic com-

Garbitsch (Henry Daniell) and Hynkel get an ultimatum from Napaloni (Jack Oakie).

Hynkel endures a dance with
Madame Napaloni (Grace Hayle).

mentary on a world gone mad. It has a solid fabric of irresistible humor. It also blazes with indignation. The lonely little clown with the baggy pants, the small mustache and the shuffling swagger has something more to note in his latest motion picture than the funny and moving misadventures of an appealing non-conformist. *The Great Dictator* is a frank, hard-hitting attack on Fascism, in which violent caricature bulks even larger than the immutable comedy of human existence that Chaplin knows so well.

New York Post. Reviewed by Archer Winsten.

To sum up, *The Great Dictator* is at its best when it follows either the Chaplin comic tradition of impolite slapstick or allows Mr. Chaplin to

exercise his satiric genius on Hitler. And needless to say, there is nothing better than Chaplin at his best. But in between times the tragedy implicit in the subject overweighs the comedy. Laughter and tears, long held to be closely akin, don't mingle quite so well on this political plane. The final speech demonstrates that it has even put Mr. Chaplin momentarily off balance.

New York Journal-American. Reviewed by Rose Pelswick.

The picture is not only part satire and out-and-out slapstick at which times it's very funny, but also, which makes for unevenness, part grim reality. It's at its best when Chaplin devotes himself to comedy.

Hynkel's day at duck shooting
is his last free one.

Chaplin as the philosophical
murderer.

Monsieur Verdoux

*A United Artists Release—123 Minutes (April 11,
1947)*

CAST

Charles Chaplin (as Henri Verdoux, alias Varnay, Bonheur, Floray), Mady Correll, Allison Roddan, Robert Lewis, Audrey Betz.

The Ladies: *Martha Raye, Isobel Elsom, Mar-*

*garet Hoffman, Ada-May, Helen Heigh, Marjorie
Bennett, Marilyn Nash.*

The Couvais Family: *Irving Bacon, Edwin Mills,
Virginia Brissac, Almira Sessions, Eula Morgan.*

The Law: *Bernard J. Nedell, Charles Evans.*

Others: *William Frawley, Arthur Hohl, Fritz
Leiber, John Harmon, Barbara Slater, Vera*

"If it were done when 'tis done, then 'twere well it were done quickly." Lydia (Margaret Hoffman).

Marshe, Christine Ell, Lois Conklin, Pierre Watkin, Tom Wilson, Wheeler Dryden, Phillips Smalley, Barry Norton, and Edna Purviance (as an extra in the garden party sequence).

CREDITS

Written, produced, and directed by Charles Chaplin, with Robert Florey and Wheeler Dryden as assistant directors. Photography by R. H. Totheroh, Curt Courant, and Wallace Chewing. Music composed by Charles Chaplin. Musical direction and arrangement by Rudolph Schrager.

SYNOPSIS

The Couvais family is quite worried about one of its members who has married a man called Varnay. They are quite right to worry, but it is too late. Varnay has disposed of the woman in an incinerator in the back yard of their country house. Varnay, however, is actually Henri Verdoux (Charles Chaplin), who has made it a practice to marry women with money and then murder them. With the "Couvais affair" settled, Verdoux endeavors to make love to Marie Grosnay (Isobel Elsom) who has come to the house with the in-

The fair Annabella (Martha Raye).

Verdoux is thwarted by Annabella even when she sleeps.

tention of purchasing it. When he does not succeed with her, he leaves with the money from the Couvais venture.

Returning to Paris, he learns that he needs a great deal of money to save his investments in the stock market. Under another alias, Floray, he visits another wife, Lydia (Margaret Hoffman), living in a provincial town. He convinces her to take her money out of the bank, murders her, and then calmly leaves.

Verdoux, however, does have a legal wife named Mona (Mady Correll), who lives securely with their son (Allison Roddan) in their home in a country village. Although Verdoux feels nothing for the other women in his life, he genuinely loves Mona, who is completely unaware of her husband's activities.

Verdoux visits Mona, but leaves to take care of further business, another illegal wife. As Bonheur, Verdoux goes to see this woman, who is named Annabella (Martha Raye). She is a thorn in his side because she refuses to let him handle her money for her. On a subsequent visit to Mona, Verdoux learns about a poison that cannot be discovered in the body during an autopsy. His neighbor Bottello (Robert Lewis), who supplies this information, does not realize, of course, that Verdoux is planning to use it on an unsuspecting Annabella.

In Paris, Verdoux decides to experiment with this poison on an unsuspecting girl whom he meets on the street (Marilyn Nash). When he learns that she served time for stealing in order to support her crippled husband now dead, Verdoux relents. He gives her money and sends her on her way. When Verdoux is tracked down by Detective Morrow (Charles Evans), he uses the poison on the police investigator. It is successful.

Verdoux returns to Annabella's home and puts the poison into a bottle of peroxide with the intention of pouring it later into Annabella's liquor bottle. Annabella's maid Annette (Ada-May), however, uses it on her hair, breaks the bottle accidentally, and replaces it with another. When Verdoux makes use of this bottle, Annabella is not affected, although Annette loses her hair. Later, Verdoux takes Annabella out in a rowboat in order to drown her. But it is Verdoux who falls into the water, and he is pulled to safety by his intended victim.

Verdoux decides to go on to other business. He had met Marie Grosnay again and had placed an order at a florist shop for a continuous flow of flowers to be sent to her. Now she has promised to marry him. The wedding is to be preceded by a garden party. Unfortunately for Verdoux, Annabella shows up there with an acquaintance. Verdoux is forced to flee.

Years pass, during which Verdoux's wife Mona and their son die. Verdoux himself is no longer prosperous when he happens upon the girl whose life he had once intended taking with poison. He

After she has won his respect, Verdoux sends the young girl (Marilyn Nash) on her way.

had given her money in other chance encounters after their first meeting, and she, now the "friend" of a man in war industry, is determined to repay Verdoux for his kindness. She takes him to a restaurant, where he is spotted by two members of the Couvais family. He recognizes this and gets the girl out of the restaurant so that she will not become involved. He returns and deliberately turns himself over to the police, who have arrived.

The girl watches the trial of Verdoux in court and quietly sheds tears for the man when she hears him described as a fiend. Verdoux, however, does not think he is a fiend; he states that wars and the people who profit from them cause more deaths than he has. He is found guilty and sentenced to death. Before he is executed, a priest (Fritz Leiber) comes to see Verdoux, who still maintains that he is no worse than other men of his time.

Monsieur Verdoux was made, perhaps, before audiences were ready to contemplate such a thesis. For this reason, there was much criticism of Chaplin for trying to make a comedy about a Bluebeard. Chaplin, however, was actually trying to make the point that mankind must avoid future wars. He presents Verdoux not as a villain in himself, but as a man who has lost his conscience because he felt the world had lost its conscience. Today, critics—even some of those who once reacted unfavorably toward the film—consider *Monsieur Verdoux* a significant and important film.

Chaplin had intended Edna Purviance for the role that Isobel Elsom played. Edna did not want to make a comeback and when Chaplin realized she was unsuited for the role she was relieved. She did appear in the film as an extra. This was the last Chaplin film photographed by R. H. Totheroh, or "Rollie," as he was affectionately called by the Chaplin company of players.

The screenplay of *Monsieur Verdoux* was nominated for an Academy award in 1947.

What was said about
MONSIEUR VERDOUX

The New York Times. Reviewed by Bosley Crowther.

Not one for sparring and flicking on the screen in these troubled times, Mr. Chaplin, the incomparable comedian, believes in using his talent for socking hard—socking, that is, at the evil and injustice that he sees in the world and aiming directly at the midriff of general complacency. . . . Although it is labeled a "comedy of murders" and is screamingly funny in spots—funny as only the old Chaplin is able to make a comic scene—it is basically serious and bitter at the ironies of life. And those who go expecting to laugh at it may find themselves remaining to weep. . . . Unfortunately, Mr. Chaplin has not managed his film with great success. It is slow—tediously slow—in many stretches and thus monotonous. The bursts of comic invention fit uncomfortably into the grim fabric and the clarity of the philosophy does not begin to emerge till near the end. By that time—almost two hours—Mr. Chaplin has repeated much and has possibly left his audience in an almost exhausted state.

However, it must be said for him that his performance is remarkably adroit and that those who assist him, especially Miss Raye, are completely up to snuff. . . . There is no doubt that a lot of controversy will be created by *Monsieur Verdoux*, but it is plain that Chaplin is still in the game—and hitting hard.

New York Post. Reviewed by Archer Winsten.

Monsieur Verdoux has some acts of comic creation no one but Chaplin could give us. They make it a picture to be seen. But don't expect to have to hang onto your seat, and don't count on much of an intellectual or emotional lift at the end. It's brave enough. It's Chaplin, too, and probably it's strong enough to carry its sombre message across the sea and across the years. It may not be great, but it's funny at times, then honest, and at the end, quite earnest.

New York Daily News. Reviewed by Kate Cameron.

He has built his comedy on the Bluebeard theme and has tried to make the business of wholesale killing of prosperous, silly, aging women a sly, rib-tickling joke as he postures and poses before the camera.

But the joke, I'm afraid, is on him, as Martha Raye, who plays an important part in several long

Verdoux orders flowers for his next victim from the florist shop girl (Barbara Slater).

sequences, furnishes the only hearty laughs with which the audience gives out. . . . Chaplin has attempted, with inconspicuous success, to mix sentiment, slapstick comedy and horror.

New York Herald Tribune. Reviewed by Howard Barnes.

In *Monsieur Verdoux* Charles Chaplin has composed what he likes to term "a comedy of murders" with a woeful lack of humor, melodrama or dramatic taste. The hand of the screen master is apparent in very few sequences of the new offering at the Broadway Theater. . . . Only in passages of rather irrelevant pantomime does a great clown of our day remind one of his artistry. . . . It is a pity to see so gifted a motion picture craftsman taking leave of his audience. Neither the premise of *Monsieur Verdoux*, nor its resolution makes communicable sense. . . . Chaplin has been said to have referred to *Monsieur Verdoux* as an assault upon the intellect. Unfortunately, it is also something of an affront to the intelligence.

The last moments of a strange career, preceding Verdoux's arrest.

Limelight

A United Artists Release—143 Minutes (October 23, 1952)

CAST

Charles Chaplin, Claire Bloom, Sydney Chaplin, Nigel Bruce, Norman Lloyd, Buster Keaton, Marjorie Bennett, Wheeler Dryden, Barry Bernard, Stapleton Kent, Mollie Blessing, Leonard Mudi, Julian Ludwig, Snub Pollard, Loyal Underwood, Edna Purviance (as an extra in the ballet audience), and three of Chaplin's children, Geraldine, Michael, and Josephine (as extras).

People of the Ballet: Charles Chaplin, André Eglevsky, Melissa Hayden, Charles Chaplin, Jr., Wheeler Dryden.

CREDITS

Written, produced, and directed by Charles

Chaplin as Calvero, the forgotten clown.

The three children outside Calvero's rooming house. (Geraldine Chaplin, Josephine Chaplin, Michael Chaplin).

Chaplin, with Robert Aldrich as assistant director. Photography by Karl Struss. Musical score, choreography, and the ballet Death of Columbine *by Charles Chaplin. Chaplin, assisted by Ray Rasch, wrote three songs which he sang in the film: "The Animal Trainer," "The Sardine Song," and "Spring Is Here."*

SYNOPSIS

Calvero (Charles Chaplin) was once one of the most famous music hall comedians in England. By 1914, Calvero is considered an aged has-been and is forced to live in a tenement-building room in London. The despondent comic takes to alcohol to forget his present condition. One day, returning to his rooming house, he smells gas in the hallway. He discovers the room from which the gas is coming, breaks down the door, and finds a young girl named Terry (Claire Bloom) unconscious. He takes the girl to his room and nurses her back to health. During this period, he dreams of the old acts that he did on the stage, and even includes Terry as a stage partner in his dreams. He learns from the girl that she attempted suicide because she could not obtain any work in her profession, the ballet. Terry claims that she has lost the ability to dance, but Calvero learns from the doctor that her legs are perfectly well. He makes Terry bring out the reason for her condition and helps to restore her self-confidence.

The first meeting of Neville (Sydney Chaplin) and Terry (Claire Bloom) is recalled by the girl.

Terry gets a job as a dancer. Soon she is offered the leading role in a new ballet written by a young man named Neville (Sydney Chaplin). Terry recognizes Neville as the composer who used to buy music paper at a store in which she was then working. She had been fired by the owner when, out of sympathy for the then impoverished young man, she had given him more change after a purchase than was correct, and then tried to make up the difference from her own purse. Neville falls in love with the girl, but she is completely devoted to Calvero.

Calvero's act flops during an engagement at a second-rate music hall, so Terry manages to get him a job as one of the clowns in her ballet. She wants Calvero to marry her, but he realizes that only unhappiness would result from such a match. The ballet impresario Postant (Nigel Bruce), not realizing that the clown in the ballet is the once famous Calvero, decides to replace him. When Calvero meets the man who has come to audition for his job, he leaves the ballet. Postant, upon learning that he was thinking of firing the famous Calvero, tries to find him. But Calvero has disappeared.

When the First World War breaks out, Neville goes into the army. One day he spots Calvero as one of a group of street-entertainers. Neville immediately tells Terry, who, in turn, notifies Postant. Terry then visits Calvero and persuades him to take part in a benefit show that Postant is putting on for him.

At the benefit Calvero does an act with another old-time comedian (Buster Keaton). The act is so successful that the audience refuses to let Calvero leave the stage until he does more. When he leaves the stage at last, Calvero is jubilant at discovering that he is not really a failure. However, a heart attack brings his joy to an end. Terry is so upset that she at first refuses to do her dance number, but goes on when Calvero insists. Calvero is placed on a couch set in one of the stage wings, where he can see Terry's performance. He dies before she finishes her dance.

Limelight was Chaplin's last film in the United States and also the last film in which any member of the old Chaplin company appeared. This film brought members of Chaplin's family to the screen for the first time. Chaplin assigned his son Sydney the role of Neville, and his son Charles, Jr. the role of a clown in the ballet *Death of Columbine*. Both were children of his marriage to Lita Grey. Geraldine, Michael, and Josephine Chaplin, three of Chaplin's children by his marriage to Oona O'Neill, also appeared, although briefly: in the opening scene, the three were seen listening to the music of an organ-grinder on the street as Chaplin was entering the rooming house. At least one writer claims he has spotted Oona O'Neill herself, as an extra.

What was said about
LIMELIGHT

New York Herald Tribune. Reviewed by Otis L. Guernsey, Jr.

In Charles Chaplin's *Limelight* an aging comedian and a young and despairing dancer probe for meanings in a good many of the early scenes, and in one of them they conclude that "all life is desire." Judging from their story and its treatment on the screens of the Astor and 60th Street Trans-Lux, it is longing that they mean and not desire—longing, the hunger of the spirit, the star's longing for applause and the street violinist's longing for a coin of appreciation in the empty hat.

Chaplin has captured the quality of longing in *Limelight,* and nothing else matters. It whispers through the music; it passes across Chaplin's face in an emotional spectrum of variations; it creeps into the ballets and the tramp comedy routines, and it flows from the screen in the bittersweet contact between the audience and the drama. Chaplin was responsible for all this, and for plenty of things

that are wrong with his film. But the sense of longing that he has established throughout *Limelight* hangs over the flaws like a luminous cloud of sympathetic genius, in a haunting movie experience. . . . One might as well criticize a rose for having thorns as condemn *Limelight* for its faults; it is a kind of cinematic poem about humanity, and if it does not scan mathematically it touches the heart with its dramatic images of longing.

New York World-Telegram & Sun. Reviewed by Alton Cook.

After the fiasco of *Monsieur Verdoux,* Charles Chaplin has returned to his proper stature as a great artist of the cinema in *Limelight.* Visitors to the Astor and 60th St. Trans-Lux theaters will find a Chaplin masterpiece awaiting them. The little tramp is missing, but the new Chaplin role creates a worthy successor.

The New York Times. Reviewed by Bosley Crowther.

Out of his knowledge of the theatre and his sense of the wistfulness of man in the ever-repeating cycle of youth taking over from age, Charlie Chaplin has drawn the inspiration and the poignantly sentimental theme of his most recent motion picture, which opened here yesterday. It is, of course, his *Limelight,* into which the famed artist has poured a tremendous amount of mellow feeling and cinema artistry. Neither comedy nor tragedy altogether, it is a brilliant weaving of

Terry is ready to face the future.

The clowns in the "Death of Columbine" (Wheeler Dryden, Charles Chaplin, Jr., Charles Chaplin).

Two clowns prepare for a comeback (Buster Keaton and Chaplin).

comic and tragic strands, eloquent, tearful and beguiling with supreme virtuosity. . . . as its principal performer, he is not only playing the role; he is feeling it in its essence and projecting it from the screen.

Herein lies the brilliance of *Limelight,* in the artistry of Mr. Chaplin in the use of his sensitive face and his supple, mobile person as a positive instrument for the capture of thoughts and moods. . . . *Limelight* is a very moving film.

New York Daily News. Reviewed by Kate Cameron.

It is, at times, heart-warming, funny, delightfully whimsical, romantic, long-winded and boring. The overall effect is a picture of bitter-sweet corn. . . . There is no doubt about it, Chaplin is a versatile fellow and still the greatest of pantomimists, as he proves in one of the last sequences of the picture when he and another expert mime, Buster Keaton, put on a musical act together that delights the audience.

But Charlie as a philosopher is something else again. When he spouts his long flowery speeches, one forgets the serio-comic little tramp beloved of millions of movie-goers and is aware only of a boring fellow who has apparently fallen in love with the sound of his own voice.

The dancer encourages the clown.

Calvero's last performance.

Chaplin as the deposed king, with Dawn Addams as the Madison Avenue girl.

A King in New York

Released in England by Archway—105 Minutes (1957)

CAST

Charles Chaplin, Dawn Addams, Oliver Johnston, Michael Chaplin, Maxine Audley, Jerry Desmond, Phil Brown, Harry Green, John McLaren, Alan Gifford, Shani Wallis, Joy Nichols, Joan Ingram, Sidney James, George Woodbridge, Robert Arden, Lauri Lupino-Lane, George Truzzi.

CREDITS

Written, produced, and directed by Charles Chaplin. Photography by Georges Perinal. Music composed by Charles Chaplin.

SYNOPSIS

King Shahdov (Charles Chaplin) of Estrovia is forced to flee his country when a revolution against the monarchy occurs. He comes to the United States and, although he has no money, he finds many benefactors who, attracted by his royal title, are quite willing to support him. A young girl (Dawn Addams) in television advertising suggests that Shahdov make television commercials for various products, but he is not the best choice for this type of work because of his aversion to certain products. For instance, while doing a liquor commercial, he begins coughing after drinking the product.

A young boy named Rupert (Michael Chaplin) runs away from school when his parents are called before a committee investigating their political affiliations. When Shahdov takes the boy under his wing, he too is called to appear before the committee. He gets his finger caught in a firehose outside the committee room and is forced to take it in with him. The hose goes off and showers everyone in sight. Shahdov is cleared by the committee of any connection with political movements. To help his parents, Rupert gives the committee the names of his parents' political associates. Shahdov decides to settle in Europe with his wife (Maxine Audley).

What was said about
A KING IN NEW YORK

Films in Review. Reviewed by Jan Wahl.

In addition to its polemics against McCarthyism, *A King in New York* burlesques the absurdities of television, the grossness of glamorizing plastic-surgery, rock 'n 'roll, Hollywood's stupider products, and big business.

Chaplin's pantomime in this film is but a glim-

The King surmounts the barriers of language.

mer of his once great gift. The best bits: 1) telling a waiter he wants caviar, amid the deafening cacophony of a jazz combo, by mimicing a sturgeon gulping under water, slitting its side, scooping out the eggs, spreading them on toast, eating with enthusiasm; 2) indicating turtle soup by a hand, covered with an inverted saucer, crawling across the table; 3) after having his face lifted, sitting poker-faced lest he burst his stitches while a night-club audience howls with laughter at two performing comics.

Sight and Sound. Reviewed by Penelope Houston.

His new film, *A King in New York,* is for me as much of a failure as *Monsieur Verdoux* and *Limelight* were successes. Those were flawed masterpieces; this seems a failure that occasionally—but only occasionally—touches the edge of brilliance. And it is a film that appears at once important and of little lasting account: immensely revealing and discussible, as any work of Chaplin's must be, and at the same time a picture by which one would no more consider judging its creator than one would judge Shaw by one of his very late plays.

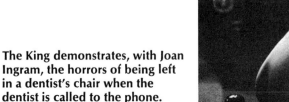

The King demonstrates, with Joan Ingram, the horrors of being left in a dentist's chair when the dentist is called to the phone.

Chaplin explaining to Sophia Loren and Marlon Brando just how he wants the scene done.

A Countess from Hong Kong

A Universal Release—108 Minutes (April 1967)

CAST

Marlon Brando, Sophia Loren, Sydney Chaplin, Tippi Hedren, Patrick Cargill, Margaret Rutherford, Michael Medwin, Oliver Johnston, John Paul, Angela Scoular, Peter Bartlett, Bill Nagy, Dilys Laye, Angela Pringle, Jenny Bridges, Arthur Gross, Balbina, Anthony Chin, Jose Sukhum Boonlve, Janine Hill, Burnell Tucker, Leonard Trolley, Len Lowe, Francis Dux, Marianne Stone, Carol Cleveland, Charles Chaplin (An Old Steward), Geraldine Chaplin (Girl at Dance), Josephine and Victoria Chaplin (Young Girls).

CREDITS

Written and directed by Charles Chaplin. Produced by Charles Chaplin and Jerome Epstein. Photography, Arthur Ibbetson. Music and Theme Song "This Is My Song" composed by Charles Chaplin. Color by Technicolor.

SYNOPSIS

At a dance hall in Hong Kong, all of the hostesses are countesses—real or imagined—forced into reduced circumstances, even prostitution, in order to survive. One is Countess Natascha (Sophia Loren), an impoverished Russian aristocrat. She spends a pleasant evening with American millionaire Ogden Mears (Marlon Brando), son of an oil man and the new Ambassador to Saudi Arabia. Returning from the Far East, he is en route to Honolulu and a reunion with estranged wife Martha (Tippi Hedren) before proceeding to his duty post. When his luxury liner departs the next morning, Ogden is shocked to discover that Natascha has stowed away in his stateroom. Anxious to start a new life in the United States, Natascha has mistaken Ogden's kindness for genuine affection. However, his attempts to get rid of her prompt her to accuse him of abduction and seduction. To avoid a scandal, he agrees to heep her in his rooms if she promises to stay hidden.

Since her only attire is a lowcut evening dress, Natascha has to wear Ogden's pajamas and whatever clothes he can obtain for her. Ogden attempts to seek advice from his friend and secretary, Harvey (Sydney Chaplin). Among the visitors to the cabin are a seasick old steward

Chaplin as the seasick steward.

(Charles Chaplin), whom Natascha must avoid. She runs into and out of closets, the bedroom and bathroom, while Ogden fumbles and fumes and finally falls in love. To obtain an American citizenship for her, Ogden arranges a marriage of convenience between Natascha and his disdainful valet, Hudson (Patrick Cargill). Lying ill in a nearby cabin, eccentric Miss Gaulswallow (Margaret Rutherford) somehow receives the presents intended for Natascha.

Just before they dock, Ogden declares that his feelings for Natascha have provided him with the first real happiness he's known. Martha comes aboard to discuss a reconciliation as Natascha changes into Hawaiian garb and dives into the bay to swim ashore. Realizing that his icy wife no longer means anything to him, Ogden decides to forsake his career and to run after Natascha.

Universally disliked, *A Countess from Hong Kong* represents many firsts as well as an ending for Chaplin. It was to be his last film, his first in color, his first in nearly fifty years for an outside production company and the first ever in which he directed stars whom he didn't help to establish. He based his story on an incident during a trip to Shanghai in 1931, when he discovered that Russians who had escaped the Revolution were living in abject poverty in the area. Prior to World War II, he had intended to shoot the film with himself and Paulette Goddard as stars.

Brando and Loren committed to the production without having read any of the script and filming took place largely at Pinewood Studios near London. Chaplin was marvelous in showing his stars how he wanted them to play their parts, but they were unable to emulate him successfully and wound up not speaking to each other. He brought it in $100,000 under its $4 million budget. The world premiere in London on January 5, 1967 was attended by Princess Alexandra of Kent, a cousin of Queen Elizabeth II. The film then ran 121 minutes and was cut to 108 for its American release. Critics found praise only for Patrick Cargill as Brando's valet, Margaret Rutherford in her irrelevant role as a dotty old lady with a teddy bear and Chaplin himself for the two scenes he allowed himself as the seasick chief steward. His part was a tribute to brother Sydney, who had been a ship steward in his youth.

What was said about
A COUNTESS FROM HONG KONG

The Observer, London. Reviewed by Penelope Gilliatt

Long passages in the dialogue (are) so dead, partly because the lines usually make exactly the same point as the shots, with the music chiming in third. I am afraid the film sometimes weighs like lead, as well as seeming mysteriously committed to repeating the most trite and bourgeois old Hollywood bedroom gags about girls wearing men's pajamas. Yet the buoyancy of the scenes that work best, and the passion of the film against conventionalism, makes it obvious that Chaplin dearly wanted exactly the opposite.

Chaplin has always celebrated indomitability;

Chaplin as the steward in a brief scene with Brando.

it is rather moving that in his old age he should assert that failure is also worth committing.

The New York Times. Reviewed by Bosley Crowther.

Alas, it is a far cry from the great films that Charlie Chaplin made, even as late as *Monsieur Verdoux* and *Limelight,* to the painfully antique bedroom farce he has put together in *A Countess from Hong Kong.* And if an old fan of Mr. Chaplin's movies could have his charitable way, he would draw the curtain fast on this embarrassment and pretend it never occurred. But that cannot be. We have to face it, not only because it has two such answerable performers as Sophia Loren and Marlon Brando in the leading roles, but also because Mr. Chaplin has indicated his great pride in it, and because it is being presented with splashy éclat. So the dismal truth is it is awful.

It is so bad that I wondered, at one point, whether Mr. Chaplin, who wrote and directed it, might not be trying to put us on—trying to travesty the kind of hiding-in-the-closet comedies, where people banged on doors and those in the room dived for cover, that were popular as two-reel silent films. But if he was, he failed to surround his story with a sufficiently clever slapstick style, and he certainly failed to communicate his intention to Mr. Brando and Ms. Loren.

There is also a brief scene—a "single"—with Margaret Rutherford as a dotty old dame in her bed in another cabin receiving mistaken gifts of candy and flowers. This cameo, plus a quick shot of Mr. Chaplin himself as a seasick steward, are the only real glimmers of comic talent or spirit in the film. Even the color is washed-out and smudgy. Old-timers will know what I mean when I say that the title of this fiasco should be *Up in Ogden's Room.*

The New York World Journal Tribune. Reviewed by Judith Crist.

Charles Chaplin's *A Countess from Hong Kong* is at best a disappointment, at worst a contrivance. At any level it is an anachronism. His first film in ten years—and the first to be shown here since *Limelight* in 1952—could be dismissed too easily as cliché-ridden, old-fashioned and naïve. It is primitive in its technique, its execution, its sentiment and its humor. It is small credit to the genius of Chaplin as writer or director, although as actor he does provide a minuscule bright spot as a steward awash in seasickness. Somewhere there are the ingredients of a happy farce even in the face of Mr. Chaplin's sententious dialogue, his innocent approach to plot and character, his cinematic insistence on head-on photography

Chaplin directing a shipboard scene.

and staccato close-ups and his apparent conviction that irrelevance is diverting.

But any levity in the central plot is squashed from the start by the ponderous presence of Marlon Brando, who can't get a laugh even by dropping his pants. Whatever the actor's talents are—and they are many—they do not include a gift for comedy. It is a role that cries out, in fact, for Chaplin himself—and it is as if it were being played by Mack Swain, the renowned "heavy" of the Chaplin comedies. It takes two for farce and Miss Loren is at a lonely loss despite the fine physical display she provides hurrying and scurrying around the suite, struggling in and out of oversized pajamas and undersized gowns or simply looking soulful in close-up. Nor is the sophistication of the occasion enhanced by Mr. Chaplin's relish for the bathroom joke or several involving nausea.

Those of us who hold to the theory that Chaplin can do no wrong must now limit the concept, after *A Countess from Hong Kong*. Let us say simply that he can do no wrong by himself in person on screen.

Saturday Review. Reviewed by Hollis Alpert.

A 77-year-old genius of Chaplin's stature, after so many cinematic contributions, has certainly earned the opportunity to toy with his medium in his golden years. And, though I found the experience of watching the film saddening on the whole, I was aware that *A Countess from Hong Kong* does have a certain historical value. For, while it derives from the past, it contains reminders of Chaplin's gifts and the gifts he gave to us.

But, while Cary Grant and Audrey Hepburn, or Gregory Peck and Doris Day, might have been more suitably cast as the romantic duo, the fault is not all Brando's and Miss Loren's. They were given no characters to bite into, or lines of any sparkle to speak. And one wonders if the film should have been exhibited at all. Better, perhaps, to have shipped it straight to the Museum of Modern Art Film Library.